Become the Force

AUTHORS' BIOGRAPHIES

Daniel M. Jones is a philosopher, scientist and musician. In 2007 he became world famous when he founded the Church of Jediism at the age of 21. Since then he has appeared in many national newspapers and *Time* magazine, and has been interviewed by the BBC, *Good Morning America*, ITN and numerous other TV and radio stations. In the past ten years the church has invited thousands of new members to join every year and follow the teachings of Jediism. Daniel also has a degree in Chemistry from the University of Bangor, Wales. He is a member of pop punk band Straight Jacket Legends, whose debut album charted in Japan, and runs the Aspie World YouTube Channel having been diagnosed with Asperger's in 2013. After a period of inactivity due to Daniel's many commitments and coming to terms with his Asperger's diagnosis, the Church of Jediism reactivated in 2017 to help all who join become the Force for love, compassion and peace – for Jediists to become the positive change they want to see in the world.

Theresa Cheung (www.theresacheung.com) was born into a family of spiritualists and has a Master's in Theology and English from King's College, Cambridge University. She has been writing best-selling books and encyclopedias about the psychic world, the afterlife and personal transformation for 20 years and has been published by Simon & Schuster, Random House, Penguin, HarperCollins, Piatkus and Watkins Media, with book sales of close to half a million. Two of her spiritual titles became *Sunday Times* Top 10 bestsellers and her books have been translated into 30 different languages and counting. Theresa runs a popular author page on Facebook.

Michael David Ward (www.michaeldavidward.com) is a technical illustrator/writer from the tech industry and is a published fine-artist, graphic designer and science fiction/fantasy writer. He has created many commemorative images for Paramount Studios, LucasArts and New Line Cinemas on such properties as *Star Trek*, *Star Wars* and *Lost in Space*. His works of art and character designs have also been licensed by numerous companies for a variety of products such as collector plates, greeting cards, custom bank cheques, calendars, posters and prints, puzzles, and apparel. His work has also been featured in numerous magazine articles such as *Heavy Metal* magazine and on book and magazine covers. His original paintings and limited-edition prints are collected worldwide and have been prominently displayed in galleries and exhibitions all over the United States, Europe and Japan. His art is in the collections of, or has been endorsed by, such notables as George Lucas (creator of *Star Wars*), Gene Roddenberry (creator of *Star Trek*), Jeff Bezos (founder of Amazon.com), William Shatner, Nichelle Nichols, Jonathan Frakes and numerous other actors and businesses.

DANIEL M. JONES
Founder of the Church of Jediism
Based on interviews with Theresa Cheung

BECOME THE FORCE

9 LESSONS ON HOW TO LIVE AS A JEDIIST MASTER

WATKINS

Sharing Wisdom Since
1893

This edition first published in the UK and USA 2017 by
Watkins, an imprint of Watkins Media Limited
19 Cecil Court
London WC2N 4EZ

enquiries@watkinspublishing.com

1 3 5 7 9 10 8 6 4 2

Designed and typeset by Francesca Corsini

Printed in Malta by Jellyfish Solutions

A CIP record for this book is available from the British Library

ISBN: 978-1-78678-090-4

www.watkinspublishing.com

To Jo, in spirit.

THE *STAR WARS* SAGA

There are nine official *Star Wars* movies to date. In chronological order they are:

Star Wars Episode I: The Phantom Menace (written and directed by George Lucas, 1999)

Star Wars Episode II: Attack of the Clones (written by George Lucas & Jonathan Hales; directed by George Lucas, 2002)

Star Wars Episode III: Revenge of the Sith (written and directed by George Lucas, 2005)

Rogue One: A Star Wars Story (screenplay by Chris Weitz & Tony Gilroy; story by John Knoll & Gary Whitta; directed by Gareth Edwards, 2016)

Star Wars Episode IV: A New Hope (written and directed by George Lucas, 1977)

Star Wars Episode V: The Empire Strikes Back (written by George Lucas, Leigh Brackett & Lawrence Kasdan, directed by Irvin Kershner, 1980)

Star Wars Episode VI: Return of the Jedi (written by George Lucas & Lawrence Kasdan; directed by Richard Marquand, 1983)

Star Wars Episode VII: The Force Awakens (written by Lawrence Kasdan & J. J. Abrams and Michael Arndt; directed by J. J. Abrams, 2015)

Star Wars Episode VIII: The Last Jedi (written and directed by Rian Johnson, 2017)

Contents

PROLOGUE

In the Beginning,
by Theresa Cheung

A long time ago in a galaxy far, far away...

Star Wars Episode IV: A New Hope

It is 2001 and a period of unrest. Rebel forces, emerging from out of nowhere, have declared their religion to be Jedi Knight on the census.

During this period hundreds of thousands of free spirits in English-speaking countries bewilder bureaus of statistics by insisting they are of the Jedi faith. Their act of defiance becomes known as the Jedi census phenomenon.

Pursued by an unsympathetic media, Jedi Knights everywhere begin to form plans to save their religion and restore freedom of spirit to the people...

One of those Jedi knights quietly forming plans in 2001 was a British teenager with Asperger's syndrome called Daniel M. Jones – or Morda Hehol to give his Master Jediist name. In 2007 at the age of 21 he would become world famous as the founder of the Church of Jediism, the world's first "digital religion".

WHAT IS JEDIISM?

Jediism is a new philosophy supporting the idea of one all-powerful life energy Force that connects all living things in the universe together. Only by balancing our self-awareness with unity awareness in the Force can we find ourselves and discover our meaning and purpose. Jediists believe we are all interconnected and one with the universal life Force.

The Force exists within and all around us and in every living being. If you are struggling to understand the concept of the

Force think in terms of spirit or consciousness. Think of the part of you that thinks, feels, loves and dreams and is somehow separate from your body. It is the part of you that may or may not survive death depending on your beliefs. All belief systems and religions are welcome within Jediism, including atheism. Jediism encourages respect, compassion, kindness, acceptance and tolerance regardless of culture, religion, gender, sexual and racial identity and background.

The Force has a light and a dark side. The light side is all that is loving, compassionate and wise, and the dark side the polar opposite. Jediists always seek the light in everyone and everything.

Jediism is a digital philosophy. Followers embrace technology and regard the internet as an absolutely essential tool for spreading the word and connecting like-minded individuals. This means it can be practised with the application of online technologies alone and requires no physical church or place of meeting for followers. Having said that, many Jediists do also engage in real-life meets, ceremonies and gatherings where cloaks and lightsabers can be worn but ritual and clothing requirements are certainly not mandatory.

Self-help is fundamental for all Jediists, and the movement offers applied living techniques to encourage personal growth and development, but at its absolute core Jediism is about helping others. A Jediist strives to remain in a constant state of calm alertness so that he or she can protect the vulnerable and defenceless at all times.

RELIGION OR NOT?

The 2001 Jedi census phenomenon began the debate – which rages on today – about whether Jediism is actually a religion or not. It is possible to argue that Jediism is a religion because it is a spiritual way of living that promotes moral and ethical improvement, which is the definition of religion. But it is also possible to argue that it is not a religion, and more a philosophical or spiritual movement of people who refuse to be defined by government-imposed or traditionally acceptable categories. The only definition that might perhaps apply to a Jediist is "guardian or warrior of the light".

A Jediist is a guardian or warrior of the light.

The decision about whether or not Jediism is a religion is one that you must ultimately make for yourself after you read this book. In many ways, though, that decision is perhaps irrelevant, as it is first and foremost a philosophical spiritual movement. It is whatever you feel comfortable with and what empowers you to find meaning in your life and live to your full potential. The word "church" does carry with it religious connotations but the word church has now gone beyond its original Christian associations and is now often used to describe a community of people who share similar beliefs. There does not have to be a religious connection.

In other words, it is actually immaterial whether Jediism is a religion or not. All that matters is the bigger spiritual picture and whether Jediism helps you find your purpose. If it can help you live a happier and more rewarding life then it has fulfilled its meaning and purpose through you and the light that your happiness and fulfilment can bring to the world.

HOW THIS BOOK CAME TO BE

Jediism first caught and held my attention in the spring of 2014. Since leaving King's College, Cambridge University with a Master's in English and Theology I've spent close to two decades writing best-selling and *Sunday Times* Top 10 spiritual books. At the time I was busy compiling an A to Z of as many world religions as word count would allow for a book I was writing called *How to Find Heaven*. The idea was to show my readers that there is a very real difference between religion and spirituality and that you can be spiritual but not necessarily religious. I also wanted to introduce my readers to other religions, even obscure ones they might never have heard of before, in the hope they would notice that there was profound beauty in them all, and that in essence they all sought or said the same thing but simply expressed their light in different ways. I even included atheism and humanism in my A to Z as it could be argued that they make a religion of their ideas.

At the end of the A to Z I asked my readers to name their top three religions and then to think about why these three spoke to them more than others. I wasn't being flippant here. I wanted my readers to see how their choices could reveal a lot about their spiritual needs, and perhaps show them that one movement can't satisfy all your spiritual needs and there may be elements in others you are drawn to. Along the way I told them what my top three belief picks were and how my choices had surprised even me – especially as the movement I found myself most strongly drawn to was Jediism.

Jediism appealed to me because of its emphasis on inner calm, altruism, positive thinking and positive doing. I also related powerfully to the idea of the Force within and around me. I was completely in tune with a movement that was universal, in that it embraced and valued all religions and belief systems as long as they harmed no one and brought a sense of personal fulfilment. The lighthearted *Star Wars* connection didn't bother me in the slightest as I immediately saw that the Force was simply a metaphor for spirit, Chi, Prana or whatever name you want to give the spark of life that is eternal. Also many religions draw inspiration from stories that stretch the limits of the imagination and aren't thought to be real but valued because they offer profound life lessons or truths.

Mentioning Jediism in my A to Z connected me to Daniel two years later. In early 2016 I decided to interview a number of influential spiritual leaders, teachers and experts for my website blog, and Daniel was on my list of people to interview. Once again my aim was to open minds to the idea that there are many paths to the same truths. I sent him an email requesting an interview and to my delight he replied and an interview was agreed over Skype. I was instantly impressed by his intelligence, vision, courage, honesty, humour and sincerity as a spiritual leader. During our interview I asked him if he had a Book of Jediist Scripture or church literature as I was curious to read it. He told me that he did have several leaflets but no book. Over the years several publishers had been in touch with him to write a book about Jediism but he had not followed up any of these opportunities because writing a book felt like an almost insurmountable challenge for him. He would also need help from a writer in tune with Jediism and so far he had not met anyone suitable.

At that moment I knew I was uniquely qualified to help Daniel write his book of scripture. First, I've been a truth seeker all my life. Second, I've spent two decades researching and writing about spiritual growth. Third, I named Jediism as my top religious choice in one of my books and everything about the movement resonated with me. Fourth, I was aware of Daniel's Asperger's diagnosis and as my father was definitely on the autism spectrum I had personal experience of the challenges related to the condition and how best to interview Daniel. Last, but by no means least, I simply adore *Star Wars*. Always have. Always will. I remember the buzz of excitement attending the original movie screenings with my family in the 1970s and early 1980s and how I felt like I could quite literally fly into space after watching it. The world didn't seem small anymore after *Star Wars*. It became a universe of infinite possibilities.

Without wanting to sound evangelical it did feel that the Force was calling me to interview Daniel and help him write his book. So over a period of several months in late 2016 and early 2017 I interviewed Daniel in person, on the phone and via Skype. Then with the help of the amazing editorial team at Watkins led by sci fi expert Paul Simpson and Publisher Jo Lal I got down to work transcribing those interviews into the first official book of scripture for the Church of Jediism – the book you are reading right now.

WHAT LIES AHEAD?

This book can open your mind to new ways of thinking and feeling about yourself and others and the world around you. Daniel shares his life story in his own words: his struggles, his journey of self-discovery, his spiritual awakening, how he felt called to found the Church of Jediism in 2007, and the story of what happened to the church in its first ten years of existence.

The interviews with Daniel are organized into nine chapters with each chapter focusing on a specific period of Daniel's life and the profound lessons he learned along the way. Each chapter also contains a Jediist teaching with spiritual inspirations drawn from many different sources, and that teaching is followed in turn by a series of applied living techniques or practical living guidelines. These guidelines can immediately be incorporated into your daily life to help you understand and live the way of the Jediist.

Your journey as a Jediist may stop there, but if you are interested in joining the Church of Jediism, or want to find out more, at the end of the book there is an appendix with all relevant information and links. You will also find information there about connecting with Daniel online and becoming part of an online community of free but focused Jediist spirits who are committed to becoming the change they want to see in the world.

Before you begin your exploratory journey into the heart of Jediism I have just one request to make of you. Until you have finished this book, suspend your disbelief. Put everything you think you know about Jediism, Daniel, *Star Wars* and religion to one side. You are also bound to have your own opinions about spirituality, but leave them all at the door now. If you settle down to play a computer game you would focus on enjoying the game and then have an opinion about the quality of the game after you have played it. Do the same for this book. Read it without prejudice or prejudgement, and along the way see if anything resonates with you or you gain a new perspective.

It is the easiest thing in the world to find fault and to criticize or judge. It is the most beautiful and empowering thing in the world to have an open mind. An open mind will take you further than you ever imagined as the mind that can open to new ideas won't ever return to its original size.

So what lies ahead? Absolutely everything. More than you can ever have imagined. A new way of thinking, feeling, living and being. A new beginning. A new hope. Time now for Daniel M. Jones to open up the first official Book of Scripture for the

Church of Jediism and for a brand new spiritual adventure or understanding in your life to unfold. As you read may you become the Force!

Theresa Cheung (April, 2017)

www.theresacheung.com

THE JEDI CENSUS PHENOMENON

Following a UK nationwide online campaign, the Jedi religion attracted public attention in 2001 when 390,127 people from England and Wales and 14,052 from Scotland identified themselves as Jedi on the census. Around the world that same year bureaus of statistics were noticing with disbelief increasing numbers of people putting Jedi Knight on their census form. For example, in Australia 70,000 declared themselves members of the Jedi order and in New Zealand 53,000 listed themselves as Jedi. In Canada 21,000 put Jedi down as their religion.

There is no doubt many who listed Jedi as their religion were doing it as a joke protest against being categorized in any way or defined by traditional religion, and the number of people declaring themselves Jedi has dropped fractionally in recent years, but a seed was sown in 2001 and Jedi Knights are still by far the most popular alternative faith on and off the census. Today, there are numerous thriving Jedi groups and churches online but the most significant and well publicized, with an estimated 500,000 followers registering their interest online, is the Church of Jediism founded in 2007 by Daniel M. Jones.

References: https://en.wikipedia.org/wiki/Jedi_census_phenomenon
http://visual.ons.gov.uk/2011-census-religion/

*Think lightly of
yourself and deeply
of the universe.*

Daniel M. Jones

Chapter ONE

The Intelligence
of a Student

A little more knowledge might light our way.

Yoda, *Star Wars Episode III: Revenge of the Sith*

The only prerequisite of Jediism is intelligence. Not intelligence as defined by school grades, degrees, book learning or the use of complicated words, but the intelligence to understand that the meaning of life is to learn. In other words, curiosity. A lot of people don't understand this definition of intelligence so I will talk about my beginnings now to help redefine any conditioned thinking about intelligence you may have – or as Master Yoda says to Luke in *The Empire Strikes Back*, "You must unlearn what you have learned."

ETERNAL STUDENT

From as early as I can remember I've wanted to know the meaning of life. I've never been satisfied with being told that "this is just the way things are" or that we simply can't understand why we are here. The eternal student in me has always refused to accept that anything in this life is a closed book. No book stays closed as far as I am concerned. I find a way to open it, even if that book is the book of life itself. But, I can hear you thinking, who is this guy? Who is Daniel M. Jones?

Well, I'm from a galaxy not so far away: Holyhead, the largest town in the county of Anglesey in Wales, to be precise! I am no different from you or anyone else in the universe, no better and no worse. I'm part of the eternal living Force that pulses through all of us. However, I am also a Jediist Master and founding head of the Church of Jediism.

Google my name and you are likely to find a "hero" with many faces: Jediist Master. Musician. *Star Wars* nerd. YouTuber. Asperger's sufferer. Big kid.

Okay. I admit it. I am all those things and the critics may have a point about the big kid bit. All children, except me, grow up. Absolutely impossible to deny. I live for and love *Star Wars*. I have a fine collection of lightsabers and *Star Wars* memorabilia. I'm childlike in my terminal curiosity. I see the world around me as one of infinite possibility. In all those senses I am very much a boy trapped in a man's body. However, this is not the whole story. I have a darker and more mature side. I approach life in an incredibly logical and scientific way. I analyse and compute everything. My immediate response when I encounter someone or something new is to try to figure them out from every angle, and then I try to work out how I can understand or improve things. Friends and family have been known to compare me to a machine in the way I systematically process people and things.

So, I'm a mass of contradictions. A child at heart who is wise beyond his years. A spiritual seeker and a scientist. A pop punk musician who craves silence. A chemist and an alchemist. A fierce critic of authority who has founded a new religion. A shy but articulate public speaker. A peace-loving rebel. A serious clown. A distracted student who lives to learn.

During my childhood parents and teachers tried everything they could to figure me out. They were desperate for me to fit in. I was always the exception and a cause of anxiety to those who tried to mentor or "educate" me. Yet, as I watched those around me tear their hair out with frustration, because no box, school, therapy or approach ever seemed right for me, I knew that my destiny was not to repress my energies or try to be someone I am not but to find a way to balance and control my opposing energies and to stand out with my uniqueness rather than fit in. I believe that is exactly what I have done with my life. I have found ways to understand myself and fulfil my potential through my understanding of the Force and founding the Church of Jediism.

I'm fast forwarding here so let's step back in time to my childhood. I was born in 1986 in St David's Hospital, Bangor, and grew up in Holyhead, North Wales. By the age of 11 I was this challenging oddball that nobody could figure out. Incredibly self-willed, I decided to take matters into my own hands and figure myself out. It soon became clear to me that the way to do that wasn't to start with me but to start with the bigger picture, life itself. I was a drop in the ocean of life. If I could figure out the ocean, or meaning of life, I would understand me.

What was the point of it all? One place I wasn't finding enough answers to the meaning of life question was school. I felt let down not so much by what I was taught but by the way it was taught. I wasn't inspired. Many of the teachers weren't interested in or simply didn't have the energy or passion to give their time to a pupil who never stopped asking "why". There were exceptions. I remember having absolutely brilliant conversations in my teens with my physics and chemistry teachers. I'd quiz them about the possibilities of time travel or start lengthy discussions about how life came about, how humans exist, what thoughts are and so on. History too was a particularly engrossing subject for me, learning about why people do the things they do and how to relate history to the present and the future. Apart from that, though, school wasn't satisfying my insatiable appetite for meaning.

I have dyslexia, and so reading was a challenge. It took me ages to decipher a book and I soon began to rely on audio recordings or family members reading to me. I spent my evenings listening to and memorizing the *Encyclopaedia Encarta* discs. I was an expert on lots of unusual things. I had and still have a very curious mind that needs constant input and stimulation. Sometimes I would have so many mindblowing thoughts firing around in my head I would go into meltdown. I would scream and hit walls or hide under tables in frustration because there was too much happening in my mind. I needed internal peace and focus but didn't know how, so I lashed out physically.

My irrational mental and physical meltdowns really alarmed my parents and alienated me from my school friends. In lessons I would irritate my teachers with my endless interruptions and uninvited "why" questions. They would give me that exasperated stare and I was sent yet again to sit outside the headmaster's office. I actually preferred that location because it gave me something I treasured: peace and quiet to think and dream. The distractions, noise and constant untidiness of the classroom were challenging for me to deal with.

And while we are on the subject of challenging environments to learn and grow up in let's talk about my father.

FATHER AND SON

Growing up, I couldn't let anyone get close to me, even my family, and I remain a work in progress to this day as far as emotional closeness is concerned. The working of the heart is an area I constantly need to develop greater understanding of. I believe in time I will.

My relationship with my father, Christopher, was particularly influential. I love my father, and I know he loves me, but we are similar in that we both have issues with understanding and expressing our emotions, and because of that we were not as close as we could have been when I was growing up. Perhaps this emotional distance is what made me fall deeply and completely in love with *Star Wars* the first time I saw the movie at the tender age of four back in 1990. The mysterious father or authoritarian Darth Vader figure looms large in many people's lives, even for those who have never known their fathers. Perhaps that is the reason the films spoke so eloquently to me during my childhood and continue to inform my life, as connecting emotionally with my father is a constant ongoing process.

Having an exceptional father is both a blessing and a curse. He sparkled academically. I left school with few qualifications. He was a respected archaeologist and historian before becoming an even more successful entrepreneur. I have never settled into a formal career and have no desire to. My father is sporty and a powerful physical presence. I'm not a sportsman but a musician and dreamer. The only meeting ground we had when I was growing up – and still have – was his love of Karate and several years later in my darkest hour it was this mutual respect for martial arts that would come to my aid.

My father was a master of martial arts just as he was a master of everything he applied himself to. As well as the physical discipline of Karate training there is, of course, the mental discipline and in my childhood and teens that is what fascinated me rather than the physical training. For reasons unknown to me at the time, joining a group of people to learn martial arts practice was anathema to me. I suffered from agoraphobia, and I didn't like to be touched or to be in large groups of people. Physical activity was another potential meltdown trigger for me. I felt safer with the cerebral world and learned about the Japanese and Buddhist spiritual approaches to life from my father's love of martial arts, and so was first introduced to the way of the Samurai and the mighty universal power of Chi or life Force energy. The concept gripped me from day one. I immediately sensed the resonance with the *Star Wars* movies and the importance of harnessing the power of Chi energy and balancing the light and dark sides of our natures or the light and dark side of the Force.

I hadn't even started primary school when I watched *Star Wars* for the first time. It was love at first sight. I was mesmerized by Luke Skywalker's transformation from a meek boy into a determined and confident Jedi Knight and my first thoughts were: "Wouldn't it be cool if I could become the Force." From then on I had the movies on endless repeat, watching them both before and after school. I couldn't get enough of *Star Wars*. I collected all the literature and toys and memorabilia. It would not be an understatement to say *Star Wars* was absolutely everything to me. To this day I can quote almost every scene of the original three movies (Episodes IV to VI) word for word. *Star Wars* was, and remains, my obsession, but on reflection my entire life is obsessive. I didn't play with toys; I would categorize them, line them up, and then reorder them over and over again. My mind perpetually buzzes with thoughts, ideas and insights, not just about *Star Wars* but about countless things, and always there is that urgent need to find meaning, purpose and order.

When I watched Star Wars for the first time it was love at first sight.

MENTORS

One person who significantly inspired my love of learning and helped me find some meaning and order in my mind was Uncle Derek, my father's brother. He was a fantastically intense and clever man. I was, and remain, in awe of him. Serving in the navy, he had travelled the world, and from him I learned about art, history, music and culture and living an adventurous life. He was also a hypnotherapist and psychologist, and he taught me much about psychology and how the minds of people work – in particular, the power of the subconscious, what is stored or locked in there, and how to unlock it.

I think you get the picture by now: I was a strange child. Not surprisingly, I went on to become a strange teenager. My parents were exhausted by my intensity and, for want of a better word, my weirdness. My father didn't know what to do with me. My mother wondered if I would ever get a job and a girlfriend, and thought my *Star Wars* obsession and indoor lifestyle and tendency to live in my own world was unhealthy. I did not get a formal diagnosis of Asperger's until the grand old age of 26, and that diagnosis changed everything. I think my parents were in denial or thought they could correct my unusual behaviour themselves or I'd just grow out of it. I think they also put too much faith in my therapist, a child psychologist who didn't seem to have any understanding or awareness of autism. Indeed, I don't think there was real awareness in Wales until the late 1990s, or perhaps the therapist I visited didn't think I was on the autism spectrum, but whatever the case, I wasn't diagnosed until years later. I had sessions from the age of five but they were completely ineffectual.

DIFFERENT ROADS, SAME PATH

I dropped out of school at 16 without qualifications. It's not that I was lazy, unable, unintelligent, didn't want to learn, or couldn't handle the exams. I just found school didn't give me enough answers or a sense of meaning. My school reports were dismal and teachers didn't predict much future ahead.

Although the system couldn't figure me out I never gave up trying to figure myself out. My self-education continued. Leaving school with no qualifications, I was fortunate in that I found a natural outlet for my hyper-energetic and out-of-the-box personality in the performing arts. I did a diploma in performing arts, and then studied music technology and e-media, where I learned about website design and gained camera and filming skills. All this training gave me confidence and a skill set I would draw on later when creating the Church of Jediism.

After that diploma I went on tour in the United States with my band and came into contact with a lot of people who took recreational drugs. Feeling high and in tune with the universe was a natural state to me so I was never once tempted but watching others risk their health for a temporary chemically induced high could well have sown the seeds for Jediism. It got me thinking about helping people find natural ways to induce that "in tune with the universe" feeling without the side effects. I knew that the chemicals and endorphins to trigger that high were already in our bodies and drugs were simply the catalyst. I knew that because, for reasons I didn't understand, feeling high and connected to the universe seemed just to happen naturally to me.

While on tour my mind was as questioning as ever. I spent a lot of time while in America studying the culture of the Far East. I studied just about every religious, spiritual or esoteric movement I could, from major ones such as Buddhism, to specialist ones like Scientology, to esoteric societies, such as the Freemasons. Everything that promised answers to the meaning of our existence I analysed in depth and filed what was relevant away in my mind. I began to see very clearly that all these movements were pointing in the same direction. In different ways and using different names they all talked about an all-powerful eternal life energy that sustained us and how our relationship to that energy or power shaped our destinies.

Okay, enough for now about me. What I have shared here is relevant to the important theme of this chapter, intelligence, because, as mentioned at the onset, intelligence is absolutely essential for anyone who wants to call themselves a Jediist.

Let's return to that theme now and remind ourselves what intelligence is and what it is not.

WHAT IS INTELLIGENCE?

Intelligence is not about degrees and qualifications. Intelligence is knowing that the purpose and meaning of your life is to learn. It is admitting that you know nothing. It is taking you back to square one and saying that you should forget whatever you know because most of what you know has been designed to keep you from realizing your full potential. In this sense Jediism is for those who want to take the red pill (to reference another sci-fi classic, *The Matrix*, in which the hero Neo must choose between finding out the truth about who he is by taking the red pill or living in ignorance via the blue pill). Jediism is for truth seekers. It is for those with open minds. It is for those who dream of becoming a butterfly. It is for those who want to learn and use that knowledge to awaken to their potential to be amazing.

As Albert Einstein is supposed to have said, "Everybody is a genius. But if you judge a fish by its ability to climb a tree, it will live its whole life believing that it is stupid." In other words, we all have genius potential, but what we lack is the key to unlock

Intelligence is knowing that the purpose and meaning of your life is to learn.

that potential. Intelligence, the hunger to learn and grow, is the key: understanding that you are extremely powerful and can do amazing things if you harness the power of the Force within and around you.

This is the essence of Jediism: the belief that everyone, no matter what their grades at school, can awaken to their genius potential by learning how to tap into the power of the living life Force or energy within and around them. You just need to believe in yourself. Jediism offers a framework to show you how to find that self-belief, how to break through the barrier of thinking you can't be who you want to be, and how to harness the power of the Force. This will involve not denying but understanding the power of the negative or dark side so you can learn how to defend and protect yourself against it, and seek the light by making intelligent and self-aware choices.

I believe we have become conditioned to believe we are not intelligent, powerful and capable of achieving whatever we dream of in our lives. School, governments, religious and social pressures have played a part in that suppression.

ARTIFICIAL INTELLIGENCE

A central theme in *Star Wars* is the tension between humanity and technology – the power of the mind (the Force) versus the seemingly invincible technological weapons of the evil Empire. However the movies do not condemn technology. Indeed, artificial intelligence is shown to be our most loyal companion in R2-D2 and C-3PO. The Church of Jediism embraces technology and encourages members to learn all they can about it and master it. (See Appendix for information about the Church of Jediist technology.)

Right now the world has never been so unintelligent and so in tune with the power of the dark side of the Force. We are told what to think. We have no control. We live our lives on autopilot. We are saturated by the online world and our senses are overloaded with junk in all media – like a constant hypnotic feed of nonsense. This is not an enlightened and awakened way to live. We need a spark and a framework to wake us all up. We need to be connected to the power of the Force. We need to be on the light side of the Force. We need Jediism.

LESSON ONE: INTELLIGENT LIVING

Read silently or, better still for the energizing and ritualizing impact, read out loud to yourself the following teaching and then incorporate the practical suggestions into your daily life. Making a commitment to those suggestions is essential otherwise this book is nothing but ideas and words. Too many people get stuck in the "thinking about it" stage but never find the courage or the discipline to do anything about their grand ideas. A Jediist has courage; a Jediist has self-discipline; and a Jediist will also live or embody what he or she believes. If you are to evolve into a Jediist you must move from theory to action as soon as possible. You must both be and do. There is no "I could" or "I might".

The First Teaching on the Force

It is a blessing to have your attention. May the words that you now read or hear help you to discover the light and might of the Force within you and all around you so that the dark side has no power over you and others can be guided and inspired by your light. The theme of today's teaching is intelligence.

Intelligence is the desire to learn and expand the mind. It is knowing that you are always capable of being and achieving more. It is knowing that you are here on this planet to learn and to evolve. A Jediist has limitless potential and is forever learning about the world around him or her, searching for meaning and understanding there, and at the same time looking within themselves to awaken to higher and more advanced levels of awareness and insight.

Intelligence is making smart choices, starting with your thoughts. It is creating good vibrations by choosing positive and peaceful thoughts and following that up with positive and peaceful action. What you spend your day thinking about will directly shape your life, so invest your time and energy into your dreams not your fears.

Few of us realize just how powerful our thoughts can be but the hidden truth is that our reality is our imagination made manifest – meaning we experience what we think. We create everything in our lives with our thoughts. To quote Qui-Gon Jinn from *The Phantom Menace*, "Always remember your focus determines your reality." Focus on the negative or dark side of the Force and that is what you will get. Focus on the positive and the universe is your friend.

If you are filled with fear, anger and hate, just let it go. The dark side of the Force is consuming you. If you let go, you are free. If you don't let go, the universe will reflect that anger and hate back at you. Far better to have love and joy and the power of light reflected back to you. Don't let fear overrule your ability to make smart choices. Fear is the root of all evil. It can grow into anger, hate and suffering. Hate leads to suffering. Fear is your biggest enemy and stops you being an intelligent student and living the life of your dreams.

Intelligence is also being acutely aware of the power of the dark or negative side of the Force that exists both within and around you. A Jediist does not deny the existence of evil. The dark side is part of the fabric of the universe and the balance that sustains it. Without darkness there can be no light, just as without light there can be no darkness.

An intelligent student must therefore learn not to deny but to recognize evil so he or she can choose the light and avoid or protect him or herself against the dark. This can be especially hard as evil is often hidden behind multiple layers of deception that present themselves in the everyday and seem benign when in fact they are not. For example, in the food we eat there are stimulants and chemicals that can damage our health, and we need to learn to identify and avoid them. There is also a tendency when we do wrong to find ways to justify that wrongdoing. No evil person believes they are evil. They rationalize it, so we need to constantly watch out for self-deception.

In other words, a student of Jediism needs to be able to identify where evil is hiding and shine light into the darkness so balance is restored to the Force. This is illustrated in *A New Hope* when Obi-Wan allows Darth Vader to kill him. That scene is so powerful and beautiful because Obi-Wan embraces what he cannot ignore and by so doing becomes part of the mystical universe. He sacrifices himself for the greater good and becomes more powerful as a result. A Jediist will always consider the greater good. A battle with the dark side is inevitable but that battle will strengthen rather than weaken if intelligent choices are made and the Force is mastered for good rather than for evil.

A student of Jediism takes an oath to themselves to always be the best that they can be by avoiding stressful situations as much as possible, coping with the stresses they can't avoid, being compassionate and kind, taking good care of their body and maintaining a peaceful state of mind. However, becoming a Jediist is not about being perfect. Nobody can ever be perfect because perfection is inertia, and the living life Force we are a part of (and must learn to harness) is a constant swirl of energy, potential and evolution. An intelligent student therefore knows that they can never learn all there is to learn or have all the answers. When you find yourself thinking, "I know all the answers" or "this is definitely right", always be willing to open your mind and add to your knowledge further by considering the other side and why the other side thinks the way they do. This is why a Jediist will never condemn the beliefs of other religions. A Jediist respects and learns from the beliefs of others.

Above all, intelligent students of the Force make smart decisions. They seek the light whenever the dark side threatens to lower their vibrations. They have an instinctual understanding of what is wrong and what is right. They know they are in charge of their destiny and that they always have a choice and do not have to follow what parents, teachers, bosses, friends or the media have told them to. They have the courage to follow their intuition and listen to the wisdom of their hearts during moments of silence and contemplation. The answers they are seeking, the intelligence and the power are always within.

Hold this prayer close to your heart at all times:

A JEDIIST PRAYER FOR INTELLIGENCE

You are a blessing, no less than the trees and the stars. You are intelligent and powerful and the Force is with you. You are a Jediist. The universe is as it should be, so approach each day with love and peace to every living creature. Never miss a chance to learn something new. Seek out the light but if you do find yourself stumbling and making mistakes in the darkness, continue to think of everything as a learning experience and look for ways to return to peace and harmony.

With all its confusions, routines and broken dreams, this universe is a wondrous place. The Force is on your side if you trust in it and your limitless potential for goodness and see everything in your life as a learning experience. Always concentrate your energies on the supreme power of the Force. Strive for harmony and happiness. Make intelligent choices and decisions at all times.

Take a moment of silence now to send positive and loving thoughts towards yourself and others. Then awaken from your rest and continue your adventure through this life, constantly learning and evolving and walking in peace and in harmony with the Force.

Without darkness there can be no light, just as without light there can be no darkness.

INTELLIGENT LIVING GUIDELINES

1. Read, read, read

Read some inspired teachings every day, teachings that expand your mind and spiritual awareness. I have a few book recommendations to get you started:

How to Become a Buddha in 5 Weeks: The Simple Way to Self-Realisation by Giulio Cesare Giacobbe. This is an excellent and easy-to-read introduction to Buddhism, but if you can't get a copy, do your own research and reading about Buddhism. Jediism draws inspiration from all the world's religions and mystical teachings but has a particular affinity with Buddhism in the way we position ourselves in the universe and space. Trying to get your head around Buddhism can be very hard because it is such a vast topic but this epic book is a fantastic layman's read.

The Complete Guide to Cosmic Ordering by A. Moore offers simple and easy-to-apply instructions for how to talk to the universe and receive into your life what you want. I talk to the universe every day and that is how many of my dreams have manifested into reality. If you can't read this book, do some of your own research online about cosmic ordering. See also Chapter 2, which explores Jediism and thought control in more detail.

The Book: On the Taboo Against Knowing Who You Are by Alan Watts. Don't read this book unless you are ready to realize the truth and change your life completely. It is all about spirituality and your place in the universe and I cannot recommend it enough for intelligent students of the Force. If you can't get the book, do some research online about the writings of Alan Watts. You won't regret it.

Zulu Shaman: Dreams, Prophecies and Mysteries (Song of the Stars) by Vusamazulu Credo Mutwa. This off-the-wall read is recommended if you can get a copy. If not, try to listen to some audio downloads. Mutwa's books will take you to the heart of African ancestral wisdom and fire your mind and your imagination. The courage Mutwa had in revealing to the world what would otherwise remain hidden commands respect. Mind-opening indeed.

2. Seek the new

Constant learning and evolving is the mark of a true Jediist. In the words of Yoda from *Attack of the Clones*, "Much to learn you still have." Every day is a new hope but few of us acknowledge that by making a point of learning something new every day. Going online, of course, provides a constant flow of new information but it doesn't register in our minds because we process online data too fast and then throw it away without giving ourselves a chance to digest the information. The best way to feed your mind is to slow down and be more mindful of your daily routines.

For example, your journey to work each day. You don't take note of it anymore because it has become so familiar. So every day take time to look at everything around you with fresh eyes. You can never know everything about your journey to work. Make yourself aware of the smallest change or texture in things you would typically ignore. If you walk past a tree, for example, notice the changing colours and textures each day. If you have a plant on your desk, study its changing appearance.

Here's a simple thing you can learn right now that you might not know. Who is featured is on the back of a common banknote? Chances are you haven't a clue because, as mentioned before, when something is familiar we think we know all there is to know about it but we actually don't.

3. Shake things up

As much as possible shake up your daily routine a little: go to work via a different route or sit in a different place when you have your evening meal. Brush your teeth with a different hand. You will be amazed how hard it is to change your daily routines and how much a creature of habit you have become, but habits are death to your mind – and your mind, along with your heart, is your connection to spirit.

Each time you learn something new or do something new your brain grows new neural pathways or connections and you add to your library of knowledge. So seek the alternative and different in your daily routines. If you can't make changes to your routines, approach what you do in a mindful, observant way as outlined in point 2.

4. Take a deep breath

Deep breathing from your stomach is a great way to wake your mind up and think more clearly. The brain needs oxygen to think efficiently and clearly, and most of us deprive ourselves of enough of that with shallow and limited breaths from our chest. Have a go now. Sit upright, and from your stomach (not your chest) take a long deep breath in. Fill your lungs completely and then slowly release the air until your lungs are completely empty. Repeat a few times and notice the immediate difference in your mental energy levels.

5. Educate or encourage others

If you know something that has benefited you – for example, that deep breathing energizes you – pass it on. Don't dictate to others, just offer your advice as a suggestion and then let it go, as whether they follow that advice must be their decision. If you find yourself eager to help and educate others this is a marker for you that you are becoming an intelligent student of the Force because you can only teach others what you know yourself thoroughly.

6. Let music in

I'm on home ground here as, along with my search for the meaning of life, music is my passion. I'm in an up-and-coming pop punk band, Straight Jacket Legends, and even though I have no formal music training, I write and perform my music. I'm referencing music now because ever since research first suggested that something as simple as listening to Mozart can boost children's brain power, educators have linked making, listening and performing music with increasing intelligence levels.

What is it about music that jumpstarts the brain? It seems to have something to do with the fact that music never stands still. Whether you are playing or singing or listening to music your brain is constantly being challenged to process and make sense of the tune and rhythm. Music is also thought to stimulate areas of your brain used for problem-solving as well as creativity and therefore to engage the brain's full capacity.

There's no denying that music can inspire and stimulate. So, what are you waiting for? Make music a part of your life. Sing or learn an instrument, or if you haven't got the inclination or time for that, listen to your favourite music. Shake things up a bit by listening to different kinds of great music, or music you wouldn't normally listen to. Just watch the volume so you don't damage your hearing.

7. Sharpen your memory

Learning new things is great but not so great if you forget what you learn. Lots of us have stopped bothering to flex our memory muscle because if we want to know or remember something, we simply Google it or check our phones, but it's far more impressive for a Jediist to have a store of knowledge in their head. It makes conversations more engrossing.

It's easy to improve your memory. You just need to practise every day. Think about something you have learned to do, like riding a bike or driving a car. You practised until it became second nature. We all know that is true for physical things but it is also true mentally. To improve your memory, exercise it, exercise it, and exercise it more. One really easy way to start building up your memory muscle is to try to memorize phone numbers of friends and family. Store them in your address book but see if you can actually remember them too. When you meet someone new, try to remember a detail about them rather than relying on Facebook or other social media to trigger your memory. Find ways each day to give your memory a work out. Your brain will thank you for it.

8. Pay attention please

You'll notice before each of the teachings in this book I ask you to take your time and read the words slowly and thoughtfully. What I'm really asking you to do here is to concentrate.

Concentration is of utmost value for learning something new. If your thoughts are scattered and your mind not focused on the task in hand, this will affect your brain power. Concentration is absolutely crucial for intelligence because if you can't focus, you can't learn new things. The online world fosters a short attention span, so learning to slow down, reflect and ponder when you read, hear or see something new is going to take some practice. Mindfulness and meditation techniques can help and you will learn about those in later lessons. For now here are some really simple but effective ways to improve your concentration:

- **Know your enemy:** If you know certain things distract you, such as noise or bright lights, avoid them. Silence is the friend of concentration.
- **Take regular breaks:** This will help you sustain your concentration to give your brain a chance to absorb and recharge. At least once an hour be sure to take a few minutes of time out.
- **Oxygenate:** The deep breathing exercise (see point 4) will improve the flow of oxygen to your brain and increase alertness. You should also avoid sitting or standing for long periods and do some light stretching or walking around.
- **Refocus:** Closing your eyes or looking out of the window and focusing on something in the distance if you have been reading a book or working online for a while can also refresh and boost concentration.
- **Free up some mental space:** One of the biggest obstacles to better concentration is a restless mind full of clutter. Decluttering your mind can clear mental

space in your head and improve your focus. Physical clutter increases the chances of mental clutter because it bombards your mind with too many stimuli, so tidy your desk, work and living space. Limit the amount of information you let into your mind by deciding what is relevant and what is not. Most of what you read on your social media newsfeeds truly isn't relevant, so limit how much time you spend on social media. Don't let "to dos" pile up. Be decisive. Prioritize what is urgent and do that first. Mental clutter gets in the way of being able to think clearly and focus on what really matters in your life so declutter your mind regularly. Meditation (see page 58) is a great way to rid your mind of unnecessary clutter.

9. Lighten up

Intelligent people have a sense of humour. They know that panic, stress, unpleasantness, rudeness or worry can never solve problems. Those things just make things worse, and confuse and deceive the mind with falsehoods. Intelligent people know that good-natured laughter energizes thinking, lightens moods.

The *Star Wars* movies are littered with humour – often understated and ironic but funny all the same. In short, take your Jediism training seriously but, as you learn how to use the awesome power of the Force, be sure to use the magical power of your smile too.

I AM A JEDIIST

Brooks Palmer is a best-selling author of Clutter Busting: Letting Go of What is Holding You Back *and a Jediist Master trainer for the Church of Jediism. His work has been featured in the* New York Times, *the* Chicago Tribune, Huffington Post, *and the* Los Angeles Business Journal *and on television shows for the* Oprah Winfrey network. *Below he talks about how the Force guided him from the age of five and how it continues to inform and inspire his work and writing as a physical and mental decluttering expert (www.clutterbusting.com).*

Clutter is anything in our lives that is no longer supporting us. It's not just stuff. It can also be activities, people, beliefs and thoughts that hold us back. When we live with clutter in our lives, whether physically or mentally, we feel overwhelmed, tired and depressed. As a Jediist Master of Clutter Busting I use the Force to help people find and remove both their physical and mental clutter so they can take back their lives.

I do this by asking people to turn their attention away from feeling the despair that comes from living with clutter to begin to look within themselves. Within everyone is the Force. It's the animating presence in all living things. Its home is in our hearts. By taking this curious look within, people begin to see with clarity. They are using the powerful quality of wonder. When you feel wonder, you are open to positive change.

By having my clients look within, I'm reminding them of their Source. This is what you are. Not your thoughts, feelings, and emotions. Not your things, your job, the things you do.

Those come and go. You are the Aliveness within. You are the life Force. You are the Force. From this place of strength and knowingness, ask yourself about the things in your life you are considering. Ask of each thing and thought that you have, "Do I like and use it, or not? Does it give me strength, or does it deplete me? Does it fit my life today, or is it ill fitting? Does it empower me or not?"

The Force is not an alien all-knowing element that you are conferring with for answers. It's who you are in the most basic of ways. It's not something you can see. It's felt as the most intimate primary force. I first became aware of the Force when I was around five years old. I remember getting a deep strong sense that we are connected by primary energy. That feeling grew in me as I got older. It really came home when I was dying of a lung disease. As my body was wasting away, I was stunned that I felt a great aliveness within. I sensed that my body was like a candle melting down, but I was the flame that was fully burning brightly. That flame is the Force. I got a double lung transplant in June of 2013 and today my body is strong again. I feel the energy and wonder of the Force in my mind, every single moment of every day.

What is the meaning of life? To give your life meaning.

Daniel M. Jones

Chapter
TWO

Personal Thought Control

Fear is the path to the dark side. Fear leads to anger. Anger leads to hate. Hate leads to suffering.

Yoda, *Star Wars Episode I: The Phantom Menace*

If intelligence – and by that I mean curiosity – is the qualification or prerequisite for Jediism, becoming aware of the power of your thoughts to create your reality is the foundation stone or starting point. The journey begins with one step and thought control is that first step. Not taking responsibility for your thoughts allows fear to get the upper hand and when fear has the upper hand you attract negative situations, experiences and people into your life.

This sounds like positive thinking but it is far more expansive and profound than that. It is understanding what your thoughts are and how to take charge of them so you become a living embodiment of the infinite power and potential of the Force.

The power of thought to create your reality and connect you to the living life Force is something I have felt many times in my own life.

THINKING AHEAD

I guess I'm lucky in that I have always been aware of the potential of my thoughts or thinking to shape my life and what I attract into it. I have always sensed that I am not entirely at the mercy of external events or a helpless victim of circumstances. My parents and teachers may have been worried about me, with my *Star Wars* obsessions and strange, antisocial behaviour, but I was choosing to live my life on my own terms. I wasn't able to conform to the expectations of others. In my mind I trusted that somehow all would fall into place and self-understanding would manifest if I simply put my energy into doing what I loved.

After leaving school I continued to educate myself and absorb as much as I could about religion, spirituality, science and the search for life's meaning. I composed songs for my band, despite not being able to read music, and performed locally in clubs and pubs. I had but one agenda and that was to be creative, and ultimately to use that creativity to energize and inspire others. Perhaps this desire to create has something to do with my Asperger's, which was still undiagnosed at the time. I have – and still have – this overwhelming urge to ooze creativity 24/7. I need very little sleep. If I'm not creative or learning something new I don't feel alive. I always have to be doing lots of things. If I'm not busy I am more susceptible to meltdowns. Keeping my mind active, constantly learning and creating, is my way of being and I'm aware that not everybody reacts to life like that.

From the outside looking in, I must have seemed like a young drifter without any formal qualifications, or a rebel without a cause, but that transition period in my life from schoolboy to young adult made complete sense to me – I was learning, growing and finding out who I was. There was no urge within me to settle for security. There was only one road for me and that was the road less travelled as it offered constant stimulation and opportunities to evolve. I trusted the universe would support my creativity, and support me it did.

All along I knew that everything in my life was leading me towards a greater purpose. I wasn't sure what that purpose was but I never panicked because I knew that all I needed to do was let my creativity flourish and the universe would guide me. I trusted that the universe would send me the right person or the right circumstances or the right insight to take me to where I needed to be, in other words help me fulfil my purpose. That is exactly what the universe did.

ANSWER NOTED BUT NOT COUNTED

I was first alerted to the Jedi census phenomenon in early 2001 by a family friend who told me about a worldwide email campaign urging people to write Jedi or Jedi Knight as their answer to the religion classification question in their country's census. My friend knew that I was a *Star Wars* obsessive and that this would definitely appeal to me. They were right. The census phenomenon did more than appeal to me. It inspired and enlightened me. I may not have been aware of it at the time as I wasn't yet 16 but it sowed a seed in my mind and in my heart.

In the coming months and following years I watched the census phenomenon with increasing interest. It made me think about how brilliantly an online community could fuel people power and rock the establishment boat. I was fully aware that some declared themselves Jedi on the census as a joke. However, I also knew that there were many people, myself included, who didn't think it was a laughing matter at all but a genuine expression of spiritual curiosity and identity.

The forces that be (government officials) took note of "Jedi Knight" as a religious choice on the forms but did not count it. This felt wrong to me as it certainly deserved acknowledgement and investigation as to why people were doing this. People were listing Jedi for a reason. I did some research and found that there had been early signs of people declaring themselves Jedi on the census but nothing like the thousands that did so in 2001. Perhaps this was to do with the dawning of the new millennium and the unfounded fears surrounding computers crashing because of the Y2K bug. Or perhaps it was simply because *The Phantom Menace* hit cinemas in 1999 bringing *Star Wars* nostalgically back into people's minds and hearts 16 years after the release of *Return of the Jedi*.

For whatever reason, in the years that followed the 2001 census, it gradually became clear to me that people were crying out for some kind of ethical and spiritual framework but established religion was losing its relevance. It was also clear beyond doubt to me that the internet was going to be a powerful force in everyone's lives. It was certainly a powerful force in my life. I felt completely at home online, establishing myself as a popular figure on Myspace (an early social networking site, similar to Facebook) in 2005. I knew social media had the potential to reach more people than any religious leader and an online community might just be the ideal medium for a spiritual message that was modern, relevant, engaging and empowering.

THE BIGGER PICTURE

In 2006, aged 19, I felt energized as never before. I'd just returned from a mind-opening world peace music tour with my band and my desire to understand the meaning of life was as strong as ever. To make ends meet I got a job in a hardware store stocking shelves in the middle of the night. That job was perfect as I function best when there is quiet and peace, and a minimum of noise, smells, lights and interaction. I also enjoyed the task of creating order out of chaos when stacking. It didn't feel dull to me but calming. As synchronicity would have it, I worked alongside a guy who I'll call "Paul" who was a *Star Wars* fan, and who, like me, had also been researching different spiritual and life philosophies, such as Buddhism. What are the chances of that? The law of attraction was at work in my life.

The similarity in our thinking was uncanny as Paul was as much in love with the Jedi message in *Star Wars* as I was. He was vaguely thinking about finding ways to expand the spiritual message online outside the movies, and talking to him made me realize that since the age of 11, I had also found links and connections, and seen strong parallels with the notion of the living life Force in all religions and spiritual traditions. The Force was clearly the missing link, the uniting factor or key to the bigger spiritual picture.

The 2001 Jedi census phenomenon raised the very real possibility in my mind of Jediism becoming a genuine religion or spiritual movement but after that it is hard to pinpoint exactly when I began to form the rudiments of Jediist ideology as my entire life seemed to have been building towards that destiny.

What I do know is that from the age of 20 I was filled with a sense of direction and purpose regarding the establishment of Jediism that may have been lacking before.

I saw clearly in my mind the potential of Jediism to awaken a generation of people in a way that religion or the New Age movement never could. I shared my vision with my new friend and he was very taken by the idea and wanted to help me formulate a website as a springboard to promote my ideology. It very much felt that, because I was now actively thinking about starting a movement, the universe was actively pushing the right person and the opportunity towards me.

Time and time again in my life what I have been thinking about I have drawn towards me. Above all, I think my desire to be creative was the magnet for the universe. I was euphoric when I researched and gathered together material for Jediism. My thoughts were always ones of infinite possibility and potential, and thoughts like these have tremendous power. I simply didn't focus on the negatives. My mind didn't give negativity a chance to take root. Research can often feel quite mundane and serious, but for me it was the opposite, and I believe my relentless positivity about Jediism helped push things in the right direction for me.

To this day I still get wildly excited about Jediism, and the law of attraction ensures that this is what the universe reflects back to me. Hand on heart, from the moment I started to formulate a structured approach to Jediism – create a movement, as it were – although there have been a few detours, there has been no looking back.

The Force was clearly the missing link, the key to the bigger spiritual picture.

TO BE OR NOT TO BE

Creating a website for the Church of Jediism in 2007 felt like a completely natural thing for me to do for several reasons. First of all, from a very young age *Star Wars* had given me a sense of completeness and belonging I couldn't find anywhere else, and by the age of 20 it became obvious to me that the concept of the Force really was a solid foundation for spirituality. Alongside my out-of-this-world *Star Wars* obsession, I was born into the millennial generation, a generation thought to be more liberal in its approach to politics, marked by an increased use and familiarity with communications, media and digital technologies.

If you believe in the concept of the indigo child – a child born "an old soul" or wise before their time who is also a peacemaker and an educator – then that might describe me. It is often said that such star children have strikingly blue eyes that have the ability to look into people's souls, and I certainly have very blue eyes. It is also often said that star children have Attention Deficit Disorder (ADD) or are on the autism spectrum. That's me again, and in addition to ADD I was also born with dyslexia and Asperger's. Prior to my diagnosis, my inability to understand why I was "weird" and so unlike my peers led me to an intense exploration of all the world's religious, philosophical and spiritual belief systems. I wanted to understand myself and find answers to the meaning of life.

When all is said and done, I don't truly know why I felt called to found a new spiritual movement but that is exactly what I did. I didn't want that act of rebellion and creativity on the 2001 census to disappear without a trace. Something spiritually

THE INDIGO CHILD

According to New Age thinking, indigo children, also referred to as star children, are thought to be born with innate psychic powers or highly developed intuition and creativity. The idea dates back to the 1970s and is based on the writings of a parapsychologist and psychic called Nancy Ann Tappe. In 1982 she published a book called *Understanding your Life through Colour* in which she stated that from the mid-1960s onwards she noticed more and more children being born with indigo auras. Her synaesthesia enabled her to see these subtle energy or radiation fields surrounding a person and their colours. The idea of indigo children became popular in the late 1990s and early 2000s with the release of several books and films and related material.

There has been no scientific research study to give authority or credibility to the idea but many parents who have children with learning issues or who are on the autism spectrum believe their children may have indigo characteristics. Tappe also noted that one type of indigo child (the interdimensional child) may have the potential to lead new religious or spiritual movements.

empowering had happened then and I wanted to preserve it. In some countries the Jediist movement actually overtook major world religions, such as Buddhism, in popularity, with the most spectacular example being New Zealand, where Jediism was second only in popularity to Christianity. Clearly there was something important going on and this didn't just deserve to be understood, it deserved to be counted. It deserved a voice. Nobody else was putting themselves forward so I figured it might as well be me.

THREE WISHES

Was there a moment along the way when I knew that all my research was leading towards Jediism? Yes, but there was not just one "ah ha" moment – there were three and they all clustered together in 2007, my twenty-first year!

Although reading was a time-consuming ordeal because of my dyslexia, I found a way to listen to books with audio recordings or family and friends reading to me, and I eagerly sought out a huge library of spiritual, religious and philosophical texts to help me understand the meaning of life. But over time it very much felt as if I knew what the book was going to say before I listened to it. In other words, nothing felt new or "wow" and I was constantly searching for that "wow" book.

As often happens, the universe sent the right material to me through a series of coincidences. (I do believe that coincidence, or to use its spiritual term "synchronicity", is the language the Force speaks.) I needed dental treatment from a specialist and interestingly that was the last time I have ever needed serious dental work. For that treatment I had to travel to a new area I hadn't been to before. It was going to be quite a time-consuming procedure and so to relax me I was given a sedative. I had some time to kill and right next door to the specialist was a secondhand bookshop in the final days of its closing-down sale. I went inside hoping to find a book to inspire me and I came across two books that truly stood out. One was *Making Time* by Steve Taylor and the other was Carl Rider's book called *Your Psychic Power* about boosting intuition and enriching psychic ability. I remember feeling drawn to both these fantastic resources and thinking if I hadn't been in this unfamiliar place at this time and in such a relaxed state I would never have gone into this shop.

When I read Taylor's book it was like a lightning bolt of understanding and awareness. He was talking about how we perceive time and how we distort it and don't understand it. I had been thinking a lot about how we can control time, speed it up or slow it down with our thoughts or perception. It was another piece of the jigsaw for me. Rider's psychic development book was an epiphany as it normalized the paranormal by showing that our most powerful mode of thought is intuition and this sixth sense is as natural as all our other senses. Centuries ago our intuition was more developed, as we needed it to sense danger, but technology has dulled our intuition. This trend can be reversed with simple daily meditation and intuition-development exercises to improve psychic awareness.

Around the same time my cousin Jo recommended a book to me and reading it triggered my second "ah ha" moment. The book was Dan Brown's *The Lost Symbol*. I'm not really one for fiction and although Dan Brown has interesting ideas he certainly wasn't on my must-read list. If Jo hadn't been seriously ill with cancer at the time I wouldn't normally have read it but I needed to read it because I had such deep love and respect for her. I'm grateful because it drew my attention to noetic science for the first time and inspired me to do my own research.

I discovered that noetic means "inner knowing or experience". Noetic science is a field of academic research that brings objective scientific tools and techniques together with subjective inner knowing to study the full range of human experiences. In other words, it is a meeting ground between science and spirit.

The term noetic science was coined in 1973 when the Institute of Noetic Sciences (IONS) was founded by Apollo 14 astronaut Edgar Mitchell, who two years earlier had become the sixth man to walk on the moon. Mitchell experienced a profound sense of universal connectedness on his return home that led him to conclude that reality is more complex, subtle and mysterious than conventional science had led him to believe. It was impossible for me to ignore the strong parallels with the Force here. Mitchell believed that a deeper understanding of consciousness (or our inner space which includes thoughts, feelings, dreams and so on) could lead to a new and expanded understanding of reality in which objective and subjective, outer and inner, are understood as co-equal aspects of the miracle of our being.

My study of noetic sciences led me to a mountain of incredible scientific research and one experiment that stood out immediately was the rice experiment by Dr Emoto, who's best known for his experiments with water. If you aren't familiar with his rice experiment you need to be. It was a simple mind-over-matter technique that was tested independently by various people all over the world in 1998. In this experiment, Dr Emoto sealed cooked rice in three jars. The first jar was given to schoolchildren who were instructed to say pleasant words to it and think happy things. The second jar was also given to schoolchildren, but they were instructed to say cruel and hateful words to it. The third jar was set aside and ignored. After a few weeks, the rice in the first jar looked fresh, and the rice in the second and third looked mouldy and rotten – showing that the way we think and speak can have a huge influence, and even ignoring something can have devastating consequences

You could say the results were simply random but for me the experiment was a strong metaphor for how thoughts can determine our reality. I followed it up by investigating other noetic studies or consciousness research. I knew I was on to something. I couldn't understand why all this mindblowing research was buried in scientific journals and not required general reading or taught in schools. Part of the problem was the language and terminology used. It was dry, overly academic and unengaging and wouldn't speak to the general reader. I knew I could help change that by finding engaging and relevant ways to bring profound noetic research to a wider audience.

It is often said that good things come in threes and the final shift in gear arrived when all the pieces of the puzzle came together in one blindingly beautiful moment. At the time the information was in my head and ready to explode. I often walk down to the beach near my house for some time out to feel at one with the world. I typically skateboard there and listen to the lapping of the waves. One morning I remember sitting there drinking in the beauty of the universe and all of a sudden there was this dramatic and urgent sense of calling. That is the only way to describe it.

Something higher and greater than myself was telling me without words, just through intense thoughts and feelings, that I had to push forward and found Jediism. I had to do something and I had to do it now. I had to do something amazing to help and inspire people. Something fantastic that nobody had ever done before. All doubts were gone and they were just replaced with a quiet certainty that I had to do it and I still have that feeling today. It has never gone away. It is what defines me. It is the power of the Force telling me I'm on the right path but I have to do more.

I had felt this sense of spiritual calling before in my late teens but it had been gentler and very much a calling to start something, even though I wasn't quite sure what that something should be. Now it was telling me it was time to get going, to stop thinking and start doing. It was my road to Damascus moment. Jediism was about to be born.

BUT WHAT ARE THOUGHTS?

In the chapters that follow I'll talk about that extraordinary adventure and how I managed to work through the many challenges along the way, but now it is time to return to the theme of this chapter now – your thoughts.

There is a scientific explanation for how thoughts originate in the brain and travel through the body, but from a spiritual perspective a thought is a manifestation of energy that creates what you experience or perceive.

According to Buddhism your reality is a reflection of what your mind projects. "I think therefore I am," or to reference again the words of Qui-Gon Jinn from *The Phantom Menace*, "Your focus determines your reality." This basically means that the universe exists because you do and because of what you think. Think about it. How do you know the universe exists when you are asleep? You don't. The universe is only available to you through your awareness and your thoughts. You are important. Without you the universe you experience would not exist.

You need to understand how absolutely crucial your thoughts are. What you think is what you will experience. Everything is energy, even your thoughts, and your thoughts are the energy that connects you to the living life Force.

You also need to understand that, just as positive thoughts can attract positive things into your life, negative thoughts can do the same. The foundation stone of all negative thought and suffering, both physical and emotional, is fear. That is why we need to be responsible with our thoughts and not be pulled to the dark side by fear. The way to challenge fear is to balance it with love. Contrary to popular opinion the opposite of love isn't hate, and the opposite of fear isn't courage. The opposite of love is fear because fear is the total absence of love.

Your thoughts are the energy that connects you to the living life Force.

It is impossible to eliminate fear totally because fear is an unconscious response when we are faced with any kind of threat or danger. While we can't control that unconscious survival instinct we can ensure that we don't allow it to continue to dictate our words and actions. Fear doesn't have to become a way of life and make us a magnet for negative experiences, because we always have a conscious choice about whether we indulge it or not.

Personal thought control is therefore not about ignoring or denying the reality of fear but recognizing or knowing what it is, becoming aware of it, and then observing and detaching yourself from it. It is about turning away from fear and choosing love instead, and drawing positive situations and people to you through that loving choice. It is connecting to the power of the Force through your loving thoughts, and using the Force to harness the energies of the universe to manifest your deepest desires and attract the life you have always wanted. It is training your thought processes to strengthen your connection to the Force and ensure that your thoughts, intentions, words and actions are all in perfect harmony.

In essence, it is creating the universe of your dreams with your thoughts and living that dream. It is not just you connecting to the Force but you becoming the Force.

LESSON TWO: THOUGHTFUL LIVING

Read silently or, better still for the energizing and ritualizing impact, read out loud to yourself the following teaching and then incorporate the practical suggestions into your daily life. Making a commitment to those suggestions is essential otherwise this book is nothing but ideas and words. Too many people get stuck in the "thinking about it" stage but never find the courage or the discipline to do anything about their grand ideas. A Jediist has courage; a Jediist has self-discipline; and a Jediist will also live or embody what he or she believes. If you are to evolve into a Jediist you must move from theory to action as soon as possible. You must both be and do. There is no "I could" or "I might".

The Second Teaching on the Force

It is a blessing to have your absolute attention. May what you read or hear now help you to focus your thoughts on the power of the Force within you and all around you to create the universe of your dreams.

What consumes your mind controls your mind and what controls your mind creates the universe you inhabit. Devote your mental energy to anxiety, hate, anger and other negative vibrations and that is what will manifest in all areas of your life. Inspire your mind with positive and happy thoughts and that is what will follow you.

A Jediist understands the principle of "like seeks like" and takes great care with his or her thoughts, knowing that they are the building blocks of the reality he or she will experience. We all have involuntary negative thoughts we cannot avoid but we can choose to think in a positive way and in so doing change our world in a heartbeat.

A Jediist can never eliminate the darkness entirely. Indeed he or she must never seek that goal because negative thoughts can teach us a great deal about ourselves and help us identify areas in our lives that we need to work on and resolve. For example, if something someone says or does makes you angry, try to figure out why. Are you attracting that person into your life because they have something to teach you about yourself that you are denying? Or is the universe drawing this person to you because it wants you to take positive action and turn a wrong into a right? A Jediist will find ways to understand the reason for negativity manifesting in his or her life and grow from it into a wiser and more profound person.

Every single negative thought can be transformed. The secret is to understand that you are not your thoughts.

"I think therefore I am" does not mean your thoughts define you. Rather it means that your thoughts create what you will experience. You are more than your thoughts. You are an eternal conscious being and your consciousness is not what you are thinking about. Your consciousness is the part of you that can see the bigger picture and observe your thoughts. It is the part of you that connects you to the living life Force. A Jediist does not seek their identity from their thoughts because they know that they are not their thoughts. They know they can rise above their thoughts and take control of them to attract into their lives what they need and want.

With this powerful self-awareness a true Jediist is always aware that he or she must take great care with their thoughts. So from this day forward always listen to your thoughts. Monitor them. Learn from them. Take control of them. Transform darkness into light and create miracles with your mind.

Hold this prayer close to your mind, heart and spirit at all times.

A Jediist does not seek their identity from their thoughts because they know that they are not their thoughts.

A JEDIIST PRAYER FOR AWARENESS

May the Force grant me the serenity to observe my thoughts. May the Force grant me the courage to understand my thoughts and the wisdom to know the difference between what thoughts connect me to the darkness and what thoughts connect me to the light.

May the Force inspire me to live one thought at a time and enjoy one moment at a time. May the Force help me accept this life for what it is and that darkness is sometimes needed to reveal the light. May I trust that the Force will guide my thoughts and that happiness, peace and fulfilment can all be mine if I always choose love, peace, harmony and the light.

Take a moment of reflection now to gather your thoughts and energize them with positive and loving intentions towards yourself and others. Then continue the adventure of your life always aware of your thoughts and how each one creates your reality.

THOUGHTFUL LIVING GUIDELINES

1. Find your books

I've mentioned two books – *Making Time* by Steve Taylor and Dan Brown's *The Lost Symbol* – that truly changed my mind. I urge you to check these books out, but don't stop there, as you are unique. Just because those books opened my mind and incentivized me does not necessarily mean they will open yours. Your task now is to find your own mindblowing book. Visit a bookshop or a library and spend some time browsing. Not a second of that time will be wasted and the more time you hang out in bookshops the more your intuition will guide you to the perfect book. Even better seek out a secondhand bookshop. There are often out-of-print gems there waiting for you to adopt them. Your life-changing book can be either non-fiction or fiction. It doesn't matter. The important thing is that it changes your mind or your thinking in some dramatic way or offers you a refreshing new perspective. And don't stop at finding that one life-changing book. Become an expert book hunter. Amaze your friends and family with your unusual reading choices. Remember, a Jediist always seeks to pass on helpful or mind-opening information to others. That is the Jediist way. We educate ourselves and then we teach others.

2. Daily thought check points

Every morning when you wake up, and every evening before you go to bed, and as many times as you can during the day, take a moment to do a thought check. Stop what you are doing and take a good long look at your thoughts. What is going through your mind? Write it down if you can. Then reflect on what those thoughts, both negative and positive ones, are trying to teach you. Embrace what you cannot ignore. Become an expert on your own thought processes. Know yourself. It is the beginning of wisdom.

3. Declare your intentions

At least once a week direct your thoughts entirely to what you want to manifest in your life. Declare your intentions to the universe. Write them down and put what you have written in a secret location or even bury it. This isn't a magic spell, it is simply making your intentions clear, and research shows nothing helps you do that more than the act of writing it down.

The idea of focused thinking having power (which for those who are religious can be translated as prayer, but if you don't like that association you can use other words such as intention, meditation or visualization) has been studied scientifically, and the message of a positive attitude improving lives both physically and emotionally is clear. It is impossible to know exactly how this works but for a Jediist it is about the power of the Force giving you back what you give out. It could be compared to throwing a ball into the air. You know it will fall back at some point. In other words what you expect to happen or focus your thoughts on will manifest in your life in some way.

You don't need to go on bended knee to pray. All you need to do is raise the power of your thoughts to attract what you want into your life. Believe in your thoughts when you have them. Put energy and colour into them. Don't just think them, feel them happening, see them happening with your thoughts, daydreams and dreams.

Be as specific as you can but do also be realistic. For example, if you've always wanted to be a surgeon but haven't been to medical school no amount of self-belief will make that possible. You could, however, train to be a paramedic or do a psychology course to teach you how the mind works. You can take small steps first and find ways to live your dreams that are achievable.

Remember, declaring your intentions to the universe and believing or expecting them to happen isn't something you should do for a few minutes but your entire day. In other words, throughout the day focus your intention on what you want to happen and believe it will. Don't beg the universe for what you want or hope for it; from now on, operate under the assumption that what you want is going to or has already happened. For example, if you want to lose weight tell yourself you are losing weight and choose healthier food in response to that reality you are creating with your thoughts. This is a huge leap for your mind to take but the more you tell yourself that you are already living your dreams, the more your mind will be programmed for success.

There is a very real difference between hoping and believing. Hoping is positive thinking. Believing is expecting positive outcomes. Your beliefs have great power and to quote the mighty comic book writer Stan Lee, "with great power comes great responsibility".

What you pay attention to with your thoughts and feelings can manifest into your daily life. Knowing this, be extremely careful what you believe in, because it will manifest in one form or another. Sometimes not in ways you expect but manifest it will.

4. Unlearn

One of the reasons why changing your thoughts isn't always easy or doesn't seem to attract success is because your previous thoughts have a powerful momentum. It takes time and patience to create a new reality for yourself. The mark of a Jediist is patience. They see the finish line but they are aware of the journey to get there and they savour that journey.

We live in a world where everything is instant and quick fix and the tendency is to quit as soon as we don't get the results we want. It really isn't logical to think that after a week of visualizing a new life for ourselves we can change the overwhelming momentum of your habitual thoughts that you have been having your entire life. Remember in the original *Star Wars* trilogy it took a long time for Yoda to train Luke and to help him unlearn all that he had learned.

So you need to approach this with a long-term and not a short-term mindset. You need to know that immediate results aren't likely but if you stick with your training – as Luke did – you will eventually defeat the powers of negativity and darkness with your newfound awareness and light. You need to cultivate what every Jediist Master possesses in abundance: patience. In time you will wear down your old negative thoughts and replace them with a shiny new mindset.

5. Raise your voice

A defining feature of negative thoughts is that they create

confusion, tiredness and feelings of incompleteness. By contrast, focused intention and positive thought brings feelings of calm, energy and completeness. We'll tackle emotional intelligence later in the book but for now be aware that your thoughts typically manifest themselves through your feelings. If you are feeling low, chances are your thought patterns are dragging you down. One way to feel better is to elevate your thoughts to higher and greater things, and the best way to do that is to ask yourself one of these three questions:

- *"What have I got to be grateful for today?"*
- *"What can I do to help others today?"*
- *"How can I make the world a better place today?"*

6. Make time

As you get older, your sense of time rushing by seems to increase, because when you are a child all your experiences are new, but as you age, things become routine and you don't notice time passing. You can't control time, but you can change your perception of the way you experience it with your thoughts. If you often feel life is rushing past, try to make sure that every day you experience something new. Make an effort to expose your mind to as much newness as possible: new information, new words, new ideas, new hobbies and so on. Hopefully the newness of this book and the concepts introduced in it will slow down time.

Being mindful of the present moment can also slow down time. Instead of focusing on chatter about the past, the future or other distractions, try to give your attention to what you are currently experiencing. For example, if you go for a walk notice the shape of the clouds, or if you are cooking, focus your attention on the smell and colour of the food rather than churning over all the things you need to do tomorrow. Be aware of the now.

In many ways what I'm asking you to do is to stop your thoughts and become aware of the right now and your experience of it instead of the many directions your thoughts take you in. In this way you will be expanding time from the inside. You will be making time.

7. Be still

Meditation is not something complicated only monks, Buddhists or New Age hippies do. It's actually a really simple and natural way to clear your mind so you can return to your daily life revitalized and with a more detached perspective. Here's a simple way to clear your mind and improve your focus you can use anytime, anywhere:

Find a place where there is a minimum of noise. Sit or lie down and get relaxed and comfortable, but not so comfortable that you fall asleep. Set a timer for the amount of time you have to meditate. I suggest two minutes at first and then build up from there to ten minutes. Put your hands on your stomach, close your eyes and listen to your breathing. Don't try to control your breathing, just observe it. Now as you exhale, picture an ocean wave breaking gently on the sand. As you inhale, visualize it going back into the sea. With each exhale and inhale watch the waves go in and out, and make your breath the soundtrack that sets the pace. Your mind will wander and when it does just bring yourself back to the sound of your breathing and the images of the waves.

8. Talk to yourself

Self-doubt draws you to the dark side of the Force because it tells you that you aren't good enough, or you don't know what you want, or that you can't do something – but I want to tell you something crucial here. None of this negative self-criticism is true or real, but because you think it is real you give it the power of negative intention which then manifests in your life. Remember nothing in your life is real unless you think it so. You need to re-programme your inner voice so it raises you up and doesn't pull you down.

Here's a simple trick that works for me: the next time you catch yourself being critical of yourself, simply hold the image of a candle flame in your mind and watch it burning away all that negative self-chatter.

9. A new mantra

Believing something is possible is how to make it manifest in your life. From now on, know that you are capable of being extraordinary. We've all read inspiring stories about people who have beaten the odds or achieved remarkable things when people had written them off. All those people are human just like you. The only difference is that in their minds they focused their intention and saw themselves living their dreams.

The mantra in their mind is "I can do it". Make that your Jediist mantra from this day onwards along with "nothing is impossible", "there is no try", "become the Force" or "I am a Force to be reckoned with".

I AM A JEDIIST

Dr Julia Mossbridge, MA, PhD (www.mossbridgeinstitute.com) is a neuroscientist and director of the innovations lab at the Institute of Noetic Science (www.noetic.org). Dr Mossbridge is also a Jediist Master trainer. She talks about the joy of playing with thoughts and references her pioneering work in schools to engage more students in maths, science, engineering and technology.

Growing up, every time I would run with a loose jacket or an umbrella, I'd feel the "lift" as I'd run and I would try to perfect the power of this lift to the point where I could actually fly. Of course, it never worked, but in the meantime I learned a lot about physics. More importantly, I learned about the joy of playing with your mind, the sheer delight in what you can discover and uncover and create – but this is what is generally not mentioned in school. A tragedy, because it is the same thing that motivates great scientists, mathematicians, engineers and technologists to do what they do.

In every one of the *Star Wars* films, it is apparent that science, technology, engineering and maths (STEM) disciplines are key to Jedi training. Just as apparent is the importance of understanding internal dynamics in oneself and others. In fact, I argue, when I am speaking to groups and helping to build new STEM programmes, that being a great STEM leader requires great internal awareness.

Here's why. If we ignore the vast influence of our thoughts and emotions on the work we do, we will easily fail at making important inventions and discoveries. Ignoring or not being aware of the importance of random intuitions, thoughts and dreams you have because they don't seem logical means you miss out on the very things that many Nobel laureates in the sciences have pointed to as their inspiration. Recording thoughts, dreams and intuitions can give you creative insight that far surpasses your analytical abilities.

I believe the solution is to teach about the truth of STEM fields as they really are. These are some of the most beautiful and joyful mental activities that humans have ever created. And as mental activities, they must necessarily include acknowledgement and exploration of thoughts, dreams and emotions.

I suggest, for instance, including in STEM homework and lab notebooks one page of reporting and exploration on inner space for every page of discovery and invention about the outer world. It can be very useful for students to write down their thoughts, fears, intuitions, excitements, and concerns about every step.

Replacing the current scientific method with this union between inner and external observation is what I call "the Jedi scientific method" and a passion of mine. Whether you are a student or not I hope you take it upon yourself to see how this point of view works for you. To develop the inner and outer discovery processes at the same rate – that is a Jedi mind trick that was clearly mastered by the best Jedi, and was clearly the downfall of the worst.

Every day you wake up, the entire universe is reborn with your thoughts. Make sure the universe you give birth to in your mind's eye is a beautiful one.

Daniel M. Jones

Chapter
THREE

Matters of Love, Life and Death

If you strike me down I will become more powerful than you can possibly imagine.

Obi-Wan Kenobi, *Star Wars Episode IV: A New Hope*

Jediism isn't just about training your mind, it is also about following the beat of your heart.

The love in your heart is eternal and is the part of you that is one with the Force or living life energy that exists within and all around you. To demonstrate the awesome power of the heart, ponder this: when you die nobody remembers what you said or did but they will remember how you made them feel. That is why Obi-Wan tells Darth Vader that when he dies he will rise more powerful because he knows his loving energy will join the Force and be with Luke at all times guiding and inspiring his heart – an invisible loving presence infinitely more powerful than his human form.

If there is no love in your heart you will never be in tune with the Force. It is only when mind and heart are in harmony that you are a magnet for the light. In my own life I have repeatedly found that thoughts alone aren't enough and it is only when my thoughts and deeds are heartfelt that good things happen, weaknesses are turned into strengths, setbacks into stepping stones.

ALL HEART

If you know anything about Asperger's you will know that emotional intelligence is not my strong point. I'm a logical person. I can understand and reprogram my thoughts. However, feelings are different. The heart is unpredictable by its very nature and can't be controlled or even at times understand. You can't fake feelings, you just feel them and sometimes you feel them for absolutely no reason. Many times in my life I have been at a loss to understand and explain my feelings, and the tension and frustration of that triggers irrational meltdowns where I lash out physically.

Given the emphasis I have put here on the importance of the heart in Jediism, you can see that the universe handed me my greatest challenge from the moment I was born. My dream is to found a new spiritual movement that hopes to awaken a generation of people's hearts to the potential within and around them. But don't psychologists tell us that people with Asperger's struggle with expressing their feelings?

I truly believe that I have Asperger's for a reason. If I hadn't had Asperger's I might have taken my feelings for granted or not paid enough attention to the theme of love inspiring or guiding others coming up time and time again in every religious and spiritual tradition I studied. My desire to try to understand this thing called love helped me discover the true meaning of life and how love connects us to the Force in a way that thoughts never can. Love, of course, is right up there as a central theme in every *Star Wars* movie with Han and Leia setting the gold standard.

Just as I found a way to read widely through audio tapes despite my dyslexia, I found a way to connect with and express my heart despite my Asperger's. The way I found was Jediism. My first love was *Star Wars* and I expressed my love for the *Star Wars* universe by founding a spiritual movement that could truly help others follow their hearts and lead meaningful lives.

DID YOU KNOW?

George Lucas loved the Samurai films that featured the epic battles and intense physical and mental training of the Samurai warriors during the Edo period (1603–1868). He particularly loved Akira Kurosawa's *Seven Samurai* (1954) and in 1980, right after the colossal success of *Star Wars*, he produced Kurosawa's *Kagemusha*, a typically grand medieval epic. These films are classed as period dramas and the word for period drama in Japanese is *jidgaigeki*. Indeed, it's possible George Lucas drew inspiration from this word when he called his spiritual warriors in the *Star Wars* movies Jedi.

Of course, I'm saying all this in hindsight and at the time I wasn't aware of what I was doing, and didn't even know I had Asperger's, but I can clearly see now that through creating and founding Jediism I followed my heart. If I hadn't had Asperger's I sometimes wonder if I would have had the burning desire to pour my love into creating something that would enable me to express my heart. Of course, it's impossible to say what I might have done with my life without Asperger's, as I am who I am, but what I do know is that the heart must find a way to sing, whether a person has autism or not. The way I found was through my obsession for a movie franchise. In short, founding Jediism was my act of love.

I expressed my love for the Star Wars universe by founding a spiritual movement that could truly help not just me but others to follow their hearts and lead meaningful lives.

EARLY REACTION

Another seemingly insurmountable obstacle for me to overcome in the early days of the church was the inevitable opposition and criticism. Early reaction was largely positive and curious but there were also voices telling me to abandon the Force. These voices never came from inside my head but they certainly did from friends, the media, religious groups, educators, comments posted online and so on.

Here's a snapshot:

"You're crazy."

"Who do you think you are?"

"Why can't you just grow up?"

"It's a movie, Daniel. It's fiction, not a way of life."

After my road to Damascus moment on the beach when I just knew that the universe was calling out to me to found Jediism, there were many harsh critics who told me I needed to put away my lightsaber and grow up. Indeed, giving up on my dream of Jediism becoming a global force of love and kindness was by far the easiest thing to do. I don't enjoy being called "odd" or "deluded" because of my love for *Star Wars* and belief in the power of the Force but perhaps again Asperger's was my salvation as criticism doesn't typically get to me. I'm naturally thick-skinned. For me criticism is just data that I can either use or discard. I realize now that is quite an unusual quality. I see how others doubt themselves when faced with criticism but any criticism I got just made me want to spread the word about Jediism even more.

During this time my family had by now accepted that unusual was always going to be the norm for me and Jediism was here to stay. My biggest ally was always my brother Barney, who worked closely with me to found the church in 2007. Barney and I worked long hours setting up a basic website, answering emails, creating and distributing leaflets and information online, and promoting Jediism in person as much as we could. Visits to the website went from the hundreds to the thousands rapidly. I advertised the church on Myspace and it was fairly easy to spread the word there.

When handing out church leaflets in my local area, people's reactions ranged from delight and interest, to shock and surprise, to anger and disbelief, but more often than not our leaflets were greeted with a smile. For me just a smile was response enough as I truly believe religion and spirituality should place a stronger emphasis on the importance of joy. Humour can be the greatest teacher sometimes and a life without laughter is a life not lived. That's why I am always absolutely fine to have my photograph taken complete with lightsaber and cloak or even a Stormtrooper or two lurking in the background. These images make people smile!

SILVER FLICKERS

Of course, we had our critics, but the initial response after founding the Church of Jediism online was encouraging, proving that people are drawn to what comes from the heart. In much the same way that when you are doing things that don't come from your heart you feel uncertain, I knew Jediism was meant to be. I just had this absolute, unshakable and calm conviction. I also started to get this bizarre silver flicker in the corner of my left eye whenever I needed to make an important decision about the church.

The silver flicker first happened when I decided to use my experience of the music and entertainment industry and my contacts with journalists to put together a press release. I knew how to play the media game. I didn't really care how I got exposure but I wanted everybody to know about Jediism, and so I thought up an attention-grabbing headline: "Two brothers from Wales found the Church of Jediism" with the tagline "We have lightsabers and everything". The tagline was to make them think, "Wow, we have to read this entertaining and fun feature". As soon as I had mailed out the press pack I got a silver flicker in my left eye. It wasn't painful or distressing in any way and I just assumed I had looked into a light bulb or something bright for too long as it faded away after ten minutes.

A few days after sending the press pack I got a phone call from the *Sun* saying they wanted to run a midweek story. They said they would photograph me in my cloak and with a lightsaber and talk about Yoda, even though in my press pack I had included information about the philosophies of Jediism being inspired by the concept of the Force and not defined by *Star Wars*. I didn't mind, as this was a great start. I had got media interest from perhaps the largest tabloid newspaper in the UK at the time. This was good news for Jediism.

One thing that I had told myself before I started this journey was that I would say yes to whatever interest came my way, even if that interest was perhaps not coming from a place of understanding. If you do something from love, opportunities tend to come your way and lead to other opportunities. No matter how I got the message out, I promised myself I would do it. I needed to make Jediism a talking point.

Once I told the *Sun* I was happy to do the feature I didn't get the silver flicker! What I did get was silence as they didn't get back in touch, but then the next day I got a call from the *Star on Sunday* saying they would like to run a piece. Having not heard from the *Sun* or signed any agreement with them I didn't feel bound in any way. It felt a bit like a step down, as the *Star*'s circulation was not as big as the *Sun*'s, and a weekend not as great a slot to publish as during the week, but I got that silver flicker again. I went ahead and did the feature and the photoshoot for the *Star*.

On 27 March 2008 we hit a Sunday tabloid complete with lightsabers.

It was beyond exciting. I remember buying the papers with Barney and thinking we needed to get home quickly because the phone would never stop ringing. The website might even crash. We rushed home and waited, and waited and waited...

I couldn't understand it. The feature was such an obvious talking point but hours went by and there was absolutely nothing. We hadn't told our family because we wanted to surprise them with it. They had no idea I was in a Sunday tabloid. It was still silent at 10 o'clock that evening and seemed likely to stay that way as we had not got one email, text, call or message, not even from my friends. I remember kicking the walls in frustration. Did nobody buy the *Star*? I had been building up to this point since I founded the church with Barney the previous year and poured my love into it, but for reasons unknown the universe wasn't responding.

We waited and hoped until 1 or 2 o'clock in the morning and the silence felt heavier than before. Then close to 3am, as we were drifting off to sleep, we heard an email ping in. I rushed to read it. It was from someone in the United States who said he loved our feature and we should keep going as we were really cool. He also said he had only seen the feature because of an RSS newsfeed that alerted him every time Jediism was in the news. Of course, just reaching one person meant a great deal but hardly what we had hoped for or dreamed about. Clearly global domination for Jediism was on hold!

Despite the disappointment and frustration, my love for Jediism shone brighter than ever. The thought of abandoning the cause did not cross my mind once. I just decided to write the *Star* feature off as a bad idea and get back to work tomorrow trying a different path. In my mind there are no mistakes or failures, just setbacks and lessons we can learn from them. Then, as I was about to fall asleep, it happened again. There was that silver flicker.

IT'S TIME

The next morning around 8 o'clock I was fast asleep when Barney bounded into the room shouting my name and telling me to get up. I stumbled out of bed and looked outside. Our house was surrounded by press.

To prove to myself I wasn't dreaming I took photos and filmed the crazy scene. I looked at my phone and it was crowded with messages and missed calls from every tabloid, TV and radio station you can think of. The BBC was on the phone, and people from chat show *Richard & Judy* and ITN were on hold, along with several BBC radio stations. It seemed endless. What was going on? It took a while to process but everybody had waited until it was Monday morning. Perhaps because the feature had the word "church" in it they mistakenly thought my Sunday was sacred, or perhaps they just didn't want to work at the weekend. I have no idea.

I didn't really have time to reflect on it all because as soon as I got dressed I was doing interviews. I didn't eat breakfast or any meal that day. No time. I just drank water. All the media seemed to be there wanting to talk to us. I can't even explain how crazy it was but we didn't stop the round of live interviews until the early hours of the morning, when we were on Australian news radio. It was the most bizarre day of my life.

This media frenzy, with appearances on TV and radio and interviews for magazines and newspapers, continued for a solid four months. It died down a little after that but there was still a steady stream of interest from the media, with the highpoints being TV appearances on Fox News, *Good Morning Australia* and *Good Morning America* and a feature in *Time* magazine on 22 May 2008, entitled: "*Star Wars* is my Co-Pilot". The feature was written to mark the 31st anniversary of *Star Wars*, and to celebrate that date on 25 May they made the decision to interview me.

During this period I felt so jubilant about the astonishing media interest and good wishes streaming in that I decided to adopt my Jediist Master name, Morda Hehol. Assigning myself a name signified my commitment to and confidence in a new life and a new way in faith in Jediism. I'm often asked what my name means but this is something very personal. The power of the name is that only I know its true meaning, just as I am the only person who can ever truly know myself.

2008 certainly was the right time and right place for the initial launch of Jediism as an online community of spiritual seekers. All this incredible interest was a direct response from the universe to the love poured into creating Jediism. My brother and I had put so much passion into it and asked the universe to guide us and give this movement wings, and this is exactly what the universe did.

The power of my Jediist Master name is that only I know its true meaning, just as I am the only person who can ever truly know myself.

WHAT IS LOVE?

In the next chapter you'll see how the universe continued to respond to Jediism and the movement gathered even further momentum, moving from hundreds to thousands of followers, but for now let's return to the theme of this chapter: matters of love, life and death.

Love is that overwhelming feeling you have of euphoria or connection to yourself and everyone and everything in the universe. It is infinite creativity and the positive energy or light side of the Force. It is also what defines our life and our death and gives both meaning.

This life is an amazing opportunity to experience love in all its many wonderful forms. We should never take life for granted. It is a blessing. Life, however, is just a snapshot of our efforts to be creative. Death, on the other hand, is infinite creativity and possibility. Let me explain this concept further with reference to my own life.

Around the time Jediism was getting all this attention my cousin Jo was dying. I was extremely fond of her and admired her greatly. Her illness and death were stark reminders to me that in the midst of life we are in death and every single day, every single moment, is precious. Knowing she was fading fast, even though my diary was packed, my priority was finding time to see her. She was a Buddhist at heart, and a bit of a wild child or free spirit, but she loved everything about Jediism. Before she died she joined the church and I truly feel that her spirit is still around me today. She is one with the Force now and I often sense her. I dream about her too. Nothing dramatic happens in those dreams. We just spend time together as we did when she was alive but I find those dreams very reassuring.

I've had other dreams about departed loved ones and they all confirm my belief that death is not the end. The most vivid dream I had was one about my departed grandfather. He was quite poorly when he passed but in my dream he was fit and energetic, and tap dancing. He also spoke to me very clearly when I told him he should be dead. He looked at me sternly and said that he could see the future. I think he was reminding me that in eternal consciousness past, present and future merge. Time is not linear.

Life and death are in effect the same thing. So when Obi-Wan says he will become "more powerful" in death, what he means is that when he is alive he can only do things limited by his human form. When he dies his consciousness or loving spirit becomes part of the infinite, creative consciousness and potential of the universe. He becomes the eternal life Force and can promote love and positivity in a way he couldn't before. Indeed in the movies Obi-Wan's spirit does continue to guide Luke after his death. By contrast, if someone has lived their lives filled with negativity and selfishly tried to bend the Force or natural order to their will or goals (as Anakin does in *Revenge of the Sith* when he attempts to prevent Padme from dying) the Force won't accept anything that isn't released with good intention or from the heart. In this sense, love, compassion and kindness are your tickets to eternity and hatred your passport to oblivion.

To sum up, love is what gives our lives meaning and connects us to the Force. When we die after living a life of love and good intention, we pass that loving energy that was once charging around and through our bodies into the universal life Force. We forever help the happiness of life. We have become eternal in the Force.

The Force will not accept anything that isn't released with good intention or from the heart.

LESSON THREE: HEARTFELT LIVING

Read silently or, better still for the energizing and ritualizing impact, read out loud to yourself the following teaching and then incorporate the practical suggestions into your daily life. Making a commitment to those suggestions is essential otherwise this book is nothing but ideas and words. Too many people get stuck in the "thinking about it" stage but never find the courage or the discipline to do anything about their grand ideas. A Jediist has courage; a Jediist has self-discipline; and a Jediist will also live or embody what he or she believes. If you are to evolve into a Jediist you must move from theory to action as soon as possible. You must both be and do. There is no "I could" or "I might".

The Third Teaching on the Force

What a blessing your loving energy is! May what your heart absorbs from hearing or reading these words draw all that is loving and positive towards you so that the Force grows strong from deep within you and all around you.

Love is the true measure of a Jediist. It is the reason, meaning and the fuel behind everything. Nothing you can ever say, do, or possess has any value for the universe unless the motivation behind it is love. Love is what gives the Force within you and all around you its power. Knowing that nothing matters apart from love, it is easier to understand what the meaning of your life here on Earth is. It is to find your meaning through love.

The word love is used in so many different ways. You love your family. You love your dog. You love music. You love movies. You love cake. You love running. The Greeks understood that the word love can mean different things depending on the context, so they had different words for different kinds of love. There is *eros* for romantic love, *philos* for friendship and *agape* for spiritual or unconditional love, love that is a conscious choice. It is in this kind of *agape* pure love that a Jediist finds his or her meaning.

A Jediist makes the choice to feel love and compassion for everyone and everything in the universe. Sometimes this isn't easy. For example, it is hard to feel love for someone who has been cruel or unkind, but a Jediist will make the choice to feel compassion and try to understand that this person is coming from a place of darkness and torment. They have turned away from the light. Making this loving choice not to fuel the darkness by greeting evil with evil will bring great strength to the Jediist and disarm and disorientate the enemy. A Jediist defeats darkness not by retaliating but by strengthening the light.

Nothing is stronger or more powerful than a Jediist whose life is inspired by the power of love. A Jediist who follows where the love within guides him or her will find that the universe responds to their heartfelt intentions by sending blessings and endless opportunities. The character traits or personality of a Jediist should embody what love is. Love is patient, so a Jediist is patient. In the same way a Jediist is kind. A Jediist does not envy or boast. A Jediist is not proud or rude or self-seeking, and neither are they easily angered or hold grudges.

Jediists turn away from the darkness and rejoice in the light. They protect and help others, in particular the vulnerable, whenever they can. They choose to focus on what is positive and to believe in the goodness of people until proven otherwise and they always trust the Force. Last, but by no means least, they never stop loving even when things don't seem to go to plan and in the face of rejection or opposition. They persevere because love is unconditional and a choice that they make because they know that without making this choice they are not a true Jediist.

If you are struggling to choose unconditional love, chances are it is because you are not giving unconditional love to yourself. This sounds selfish but it is not. You can't give to others what you don't have yourself, so loving yourself is your starting point as a Jediist. As this teaching draws to a close make this moment a fresh start for you. Forgive yourself for any perceived weaknesses you have and focus on your strengths. Recognize that the power of the living life Force flows through you and that you are a totally unique miracle. There will never be another Jediist like you on this planet again. Celebrate who you are because you are unrepeatable, and if you simply make the choice to be guided by love from this day forward you are powerful beyond measure.

Say this Jediist declaration out loud:

I am a Jediist. I am patient. I am kind. I do not envy. I do not boast. I am not rude or self-seeking or easily angered. I do not hold grudges. I turn away from the darkness and rejoice in the light. I protect and help others and, however many setbacks I encounter, I focus on the good in myself and others. I never stop trusting, hoping and believing in the supreme power of love. I am a Jediist.

With this declaration commit yourself to the Force and from this day forward may you be forever inspired and guided by the light of love within you. How will you know when love is guiding you? You will know because your first impulse will be to share your love and help others in any way you can. You will know because you will be blessed with the most precious of all gifts in this life – spontaneous feelings of creativity and joy for no reason other than because you are alive and connecting to the Force through your heart.

A JEDIIST PRAYER FOR ETERNAL LOVE

May the love within you guide you and strengthen the power of the Force for all eternity. May you know that if there was a bond of love between two people, death does not exist because love is eternal. If a loved one dies, mourn their physical passing but in the words of that well-known Mary Frye meditation, which Jediism endorses, don't weep beside their graves or memorials. They are not there. They are not gone. They are in the wind that blows, in the gentle snow and showers of rain. They are in the fields and flowers. They are in the sunrise and sunset and the passing clouds and the light of the moon. They are in the stars. They are in the birds that sing. They are in moments of quiet bliss. They are in everything that is lovely and heartfelt. So do not weep beside their graves or memorials. They are not there. They have not gone. They have become the Force and the Force is eternally alive within and all around you.

LIVING WITH LOVE GUIDELINES

1. Read a heartfelt book

Three books stand out for me when it comes to books that celebrate the beauty and power of the heart to shape your destiny. The first is called *The Path to Love: Spiritual Strategies for Healing* by Deepak Chopra. The inspiration and practical advice this book offers is timeless as it takes you by the hand and guides you though the process of learning how to love yourself and others. Equally inspirational is James Smith's *You*

Are What You Love: The Spiritual Power of Habit. This book shows that who and what we devote our energies to shapes our hearts and thus our lives. The final book is *The Power of the Heart: Finding Your True Purpose in Life* by Baptist de Pape; the title of the book is self-explanatory.

2. Live in the now

The best way to connect with your heart is to live in the now. The power of the present moment is in the power of your heart and of being aware that it beats. All the answers are in your heart, and the more you think of your heart as one eternal present moment, the better you can connect to the voice of your heart.

Your heart speaks to you in two ways: through your feelings, of course, but also through the way it beats. Recent scientific research has shown that when you feel positive and loving, your heart beats in a calm way, indicating that your heart and your body are in harmony. Obviously, hate, fear and negativity have the opposite effect. So when you connect with and listen to your heart in the present moment and feel the love, you are mentally, physically and spirituality at one with the Force.

So find as many ways as you can to connect with your heart in the present. Seize the moment – right now. You don't necessarily have to do important or great things. A heartfelt life is often about those precious moments of laughter, love and light that give life a glow, rather than major events. It is about mindfully watching a glorious sunrise, or glimpsing the magic of a rainbow, or an enchanting moonlit night. It is a walk in the park, the hug of a loved one, dancing in the rain, or a good conversation or book. It is about all those things which appear trivial but put together create a beautiful life.

3. Follow your heart

Follow your heart wherever it goes. Don't think that you will lose your way. The heart instinctively or intuitively seeks the light and will guide you there. To see the world through the vision of your heart, close your eyes right now and open them. See love coming from yourself and everything. Even if you see things that are dirty or sad or conflicted, see love trying to find a way in. Make a choice to shift your perspective or perception from one of fear to one of love. I'm asking you to do this because it will show you that so many of the problems we face in our lives are because we try to seek love outside ourselves rather than start from within. You don't need to seek love, because your heart is love already. Your beating heart can always choose love in any moment.

4. Look into your own eyes

You will have noticed that the last exercise asked you to begin by seeing love coming from within yourself. If you struggle with that concept, this exercise might be able to help.

At least once a day from now on find some time on your own with a mirror and just stand there. Look at yourself for a few seconds. Rarely do we really look deep into our own eyes so don't worry if you feel uncomfortable at first. That's totally normal.

After a few moments whisper or say out loud to yourself – maintaining that eye contact – "I love you" and then say your full name. So I would say, "I love you Daniel M. Jones." You will feel absurd at first, but give it a try and notice the energy rush after you have said it. Notice any feelings, negative and positive, that you have about yourself and then let them go and move on with your day.

You will feel ridiculous doing this at first but give it a try every day for at least a few weeks and it will soon become a habit, or better still a sacred ritual. The world will feel a much more loving and accepting place towards you, but in fact it's your thinking about yourself that has changed the world around you. Remember, the previous chapter was all about your thoughts becoming your reality, so the more loving thoughts you have within, the more loving the outside world will be towards you.

5. Trust your heart

Following your heart isn't quite the same as trusting your heart. Following your heart will take you to where you need to be, or show you what your potential is, but trusting your heart is pouring love into what you think, say and do. The universe responds to what comes from the heart. To help you trust your heart, here are a couple of suggestions.

Wisdom from the heart will never make you feel anxious or diminished. It will feel calm and empowered. There will be a sense of "just knowing" that doesn't require long drawn-out explanations. Wisdom that comes from the place of fear will be quite the opposite. It will put you down and conjure up worst-case scenarios in your mind. There will be endless chatter and explanations in your head. If you feel that you can't get to a place of peace and calm, that is because you aren't tuning into and connecting to your heart. The meditation and mindfulness techniques in this book on pages 58–9 will help you find that calm centre you need.

If you are drawn to a more technological option you might want to check out an amazing app designed by Jediist Master Dr Julia Mossbridge called Choice Compass at www.choicecompass.com. This app is fairly easy to use and records the beating of your heart to help you make the right choices. You think about a choice you want to make for a set period of time and then for another set period of time you think about not making that decision. The app will record your heartbeat and tell you what your heart wants you to do.

Remember, when your heart is full of love you have become one with the Force. So, listen carefully to the beat of your heart because that is the Force working within you. Even if you are in pain, tune into your heart for inspiration and guidance – it truly does know what is right for you.

6. Reach out

You will know when your heart is flowing with the power of love and connecting you to the Force because your natural instinct will be to help others. Helping others becomes an expression of your heart. You will begin to see that we are all interconnected by the Force and that the suffering of others is your own suffering. Reaching out and helping others for no reason than because you feel love and empathy for your fellow human beings is the way of the Jediist.

Small acts – such as holding a door open for the person behind, or asking someone how they are before a conversation begins and then actually listening to what they say, or simply smiling and saying thank you – are just as significant as doing volunteer work or donating to charity if you haven't the time or money for that. For example, once I found some cash on the floor in a supermarket and handed it in to the desk. They looked at me as if I had ten heads but I didn't want to take the cash in case it was truly a big deal to the person who had lost it. Perhaps it was to pay for some vital medication? Perhaps it was the final instalment of their rent they had worked hard to earn? I was told that if nobody claimed it in six weeks the money would be mine and they asked for my name and address. Somebody did claim the money because I was never contacted, so in my heart I know I did the right thing by that person. I also hope my act of compassion inspired that person to behave in the same way if they were faced with a similar situation.

Acts of love, and of compassion and kindness, which are both byproducts of love, don't just inspire and comfort the recipient. There is a wider effect on anyone who observes or hears about it. Think about it. It makes you feel good, doesn't it, when you see a teenager give up their seat for an elderly person? You feel there is hope for human nature and you are more likely to be compassionate to someone during your day.

In this way one simple act of loving kindness is contagious. It has a ripple effect, bringing light into people's hearts and the universe, one person at a time, starting with you. A crucial part of Jediist training is helping others, not just now and again but every single day. There are no half measures. A Jediist is always a light and a guide to others. They dedicate their lives to becoming a force of love, kindness and compassion in the universe. A Jediist knows that they don't need to wait another moment before starting to improve the world.

I AM A JEDIIST

Legendary science fiction artist, internationally renowned for his paintings of the cosmos, Michael David Ward (michaeldavidward.com) has created commemorative Star Wars *works for LucasArts and Paramount Studios and is Jediist Master of art for the Church of Jediism. He also designed the stunning cover for this book. Here he talks about what the Force means to him and how it pertains to love, life and death.*

When the sensational movie *Star Wars* was first introduced to the world in 1977, we felt a tremor in the collective human psyche. And even though most didn't know it at the time, we had been introduced to a deep metaphysical truth, that while it seemed contemporary, it had in fact been discovered and understood ages ago by many enlightened seekers exploring the ontological nature of reality and our own being. That truth, as it was described to us by the iconic character Obi-Wan, was referred to as the "Force".

But what is the Force, and why is it significant to us as humans, and how does it pertain to the most existential and meaningful aspects of our lives such as love, life, and ultimately, death?

Obi-Wan described the Force as "an energy field created by all living things. It surrounds us, penetrates us, and binds the galaxy together." When pondering this description, one might make the observation that it might also be used to describe another important property of ontology – consciousness. In fact, I believe that the Force and consciousness are one and the same thing; an intelligent, organized, energetic potential. Not only are they fundamental to all living things but, surprisingly, what science is discovering about them holds the key to understanding the nature of reality itself.

We have been taught all of our lives – and our everyday experience seems to support it – that we live in a physical universe; that everything is made of matter. This is referred to as "Materialism", a tenet derived from the Greek philosopher Democritus – who, over two thousand years ago, coined the word "atom", which he used to describe the constituent physical particles that comprised matter. But other philosophers from Greece and India put forth another view of the world around us, which is generally referred to as "Idealism". This view attributed our reality as that conjured up within a mental landscape, or a conscious mind in which forms and ideas reside, ones we construe or interpret to be physical things; in other words, the world and universe in which we find ourselves. In this view, one might also say, the constituent material of reality, the ground-state of being, is not matter, but consciousness, or the Force, out of which all things arise.

Of course, these two views appear antithetical to one another. Either reality is made up of physical stuff, or it is a kind of dream within a larger mind, like philosophies such as Buddhism also describe. Shockingly, quantum physics has revealed empirical evidence that particles at the quantum level not only appear empty, but they exist as wave probabilities, as statistical information, until they are measured or observed; a kind of virtual reality! This cannot help but bring up a famous philosophical question: "If a tree falls in a forest and there's no one there to hear it, does it make a sound?" Well, according to quantum physics, without an observer, not only will there be no sound, but perhaps not even a tree or a forest. Such is the power and significance of consciousness, or the Force.

Legendary physicist Max Planck, the father of quantum physics, demonstrated the general misconception we have of matter and the atom, which was once regarded as its most fundamental particle: "As a man who has devoted his whole life to the most clear-headed science, to the study of matter, I can tell you as a result of my research about atoms this much: There is no matter as such. All matter originates and exists only by virtue of a force which brings the particle of an atom to vibration and holds this most minute solar system of the atom together. We must assume behind this force the existence of a conscious (...) mind. This mind is the matrix of all matter."

Max Planck had presciently used the word "Force" as it relates to material reality long before there was a *Star Wars*! But it was the brilliant mind of George Lucas that astutely emblazoned this profound insight onto our psyches that we have now discovered to be a profound truth of existence.

Applying this perspective and understanding to the questions of love, life and death, we may now consider that this Force, this ocean of awareness, is the medium in which we as material beings are being precipitated, or expressed, much in the same way that the effect of observation at the quantum level collapses the wave-state of infinite potential into individual points in space/time that we call particles. And considering that the Force is fundamental, eternal and is the fabric that comprises and connects all things, then we may also infer that we too are fundamental, eternal and interconnected; as above, so below.

Life is but one form that the Force takes on out of infinite possibilities, and love is the sense of wholeness and interconnectedness that life experiences as an attribute of the Force matrix. And finally, death – a transition from one form to another – is merely an illusion as perceived within the misconception of materialism, for we now know that consciousness, or the Force, are who and what we truly are; timeless and eternal.

*Even though
your heart is on your
left it is always right.
Listen to it. Follow it.
Always think, say and
do loving things.*

Daniel M. Jones

Chapter
FOUR

The Force Theory

The Force is what gives a Jedi his power. It's an energy field created by all living things. It surrounds us and penetrates us. It binds the galaxy together.

Obi-Wan Kenobi, *Star Wars Episode IV: A New Hope*

It's impossible to understand the Force with words alone. You need to think about and feel the Force before you can begin to understand it, and that's why in previous chapters I've placed so much emphasis on exploring and understanding your mind and heart. Thinking and feeling the Force has been the defining feature of my entire life and most especially after 2007/8 when I founded the Church of Jediism. Requests for media appearances and questions about how to join the church just kept on flooding in.

FEELING THE FORCE

Appearing in a Sunday tabloid was the start of a two-year period of insatiable interest in Jediism. The movement began to gather real momentum. I worked around the clock doing interviews on TV and radio and for magazines and online. I was like a machine and my family wondered how I could keep going. However, I thrive on constant stimulation. It is my natural state. Via a hastily constructed website I sent out information and training guidelines and handbooks to all who asked, and tens of thousands joined my church, the first digital-only church. We had no central building. I recorded teachings and lectures and posted them online. It was incredible to watch the reaction and to see that Jediism, even if people didn't agree with it, was actually getting people to talk about what really matters in life: the true meaning of it. I felt the Force working through me.

The handbooks I sent out contained the guiding principles of Jediism. Not being a writer and limited in expression by my dyslexia, I do remember at the time wishing that one day Jediism could be presented in a more professional way. It took a good ten years for that dream to come true but now you are reading this book, which again is the Force at work responding to a request from my heart. At the time I simply did my best with my limited resources and gave what I could to all who reached out to me. I was also blessed to have some amazing volunteers helping me. That has been a repeated blessing for Jediism: people just appear to offer help and support when it is needed. It should not surprise me, though, as a true Jediist is someone who helps spontaneously from the heart.

Riding the wave of media interest in Jediism, devoting my time and energy to spreading the word, was a natural high for me. It was pure bliss every time I did an interview and it went well, or someone reached out to me online and said their minds and hearts were being opened to the idea of the Force at work in their lives, or someone signed up for the church. In those moments of euphoria I was feeling the Force more intensely than ever.

BECOMING THE FORCE

From time to time we all experience a higher state of consciousness when a deep and profound inner peace settles upon us and for a moment the world is a place of unspeakable ecstasy where everyone and everything pulsates with a life force. We feel like we are at one with everyone and everything and the world is a loving place. We may even become aware of a higher force than ourselves encompassing everyone and everything. We have that beautiful feeling of connectivity and sense how everything and everyone is one.

During these incredible moments we feel like we see the world from a higher perspective. It is as if a blindfold has been removed to reveal what life truly is. I think every new mother or father will have glimpsed this awareness in a quiet moment alone with her or his newborn baby. Others may experience it when they fall in love or when the beauty of the natural world takes their breath away. The trigger may be meditation, art, music or yoga or during sex, sport or exercise – or there may be no trigger at all, just a moment of profound spiritual awareness.

Jediism teaches that we are spiritual beings having a human experience, not human beings having a spiritual experience. Therefore, our ordinary consciousness or perception of reality is the illusion here; peak experience when we connect to the Force is our real level of awareness because spirit, the Force, is our real home.

During those early years I felt the Force flow strongly through me but it wasn't all euphoria. There were some very tough times too and perhaps the toughest was my brother Barney leaving the church.

SAYING GOODBYE

In early 2009, after much soul-searching, Barney made the decision to leave the Church of Jediism. It was a huge loss and in the years ahead I would often miss him greatly and feel very alone in my role as church leader. From the very start Barney had shared my passion for Jediism. His love and respect for the movement gave me tremendous strength and courage, but he reassessed his priorities and realized that life was calling him to follow another path, a path that felt clearer for him. I knew that nothing I could say or do would change his mind and it was a dark day when he folded away his cloak and lightsaber.

Barney felt it was his time to discover himself and move on, but by handing all responsibility for Jediism over to me you could also say his departure was a rite of passage. I became the sole leader of the Church of Jediism. Barney's departure was my chance to become my own source of strength and support rather than relying on him.

If ever there was a moment to give up my dream, Barney leaving was that moment. I didn't give up, though, and the reason I didn't was my heart. I loved everything about Jediism and knew it could help people, and if you love something you follow it and devote yourself to it, even when times are tough, things don't make sense, or people don't support you. You don't give up on it.

I was also starting to get some incredibly supportive messages from people all over the globe who understood perfectly what I was trying to do and wanted to help me, as well as endless requests from people who didn't understand

Jediism but wanted to learn more about it. They were disillusioned with religion and frustrated by the vagueness of the New Age movement and wanted structure and spiritual guidance to help them feel more in control of their lives. Every time I read their messages or requests for guidance from me I got a surge of strength from the inside out, and that surge of strength didn't ever start in my head, it always started in my chest. The reason I felt strength from the inside out is because love is what feeds the living life Force within us. If your life is starved of love, your connection to the Force is weak, but with love that connection is strong.

I carried on promoting the church like a man possessed. I lived and breathed Jediism. It gave my life true meaning and I sincerely wanted to help others find their meaning too through Jediism.

"DO YOU KNOW WHO I AM?"

Even though there was one less pair of hands to answer messages and spread the word, the Force remained strong for Jediism. It was strong within me too, even though I did start to notice that press reaction wasn't quite as supportive or light-hearted as it had been when I first appeared on the scene. At times it felt hostile, as if they had built me up and were now starting to knock me down.

Unconsciously, I played into their hands. With Jediism a talking point, and finding myself its willing spokesperson, there were times when my ego threatened to sabotage my harmonious relationship with the Force within and around me. My ego loved the attention I was getting. I enjoyed people seeking my advice. Being asked for autographs as Jediist Master and founder of the Church of Jediism was such an ego boost. On occasions I know I lost sight of the importance of humility and diplomacy and peace for those who wish to walk in harmony with Force.

I never let my ego take over completely but in the early years of the church I got dangerously close to that, and would often respond sharply and defensively to criticism. Interestingly, though, it was never with the press that I totally lost my cool; it was typically when I was in communication with those I should have felt closest to – other Jedi groups.

As far as I was aware when I founded the Church of Jediism there were no other Jedi organizations. I believe I was the first to form an online group of note in 2007 via my website and Myspace. However, it soon became apparent that other groups were rapidly forming online. Perhaps some of them were inspired by the example of my church and wanting to set up their own brand of Jediism, or perhaps it was simply a case of like minds and they weren't aware of what I was doing.

I truly don't know and don't really care who or what came first, but what I do know is that when some of them got in touch to criticize my teachings or accuse me of stealing their thunder I'd hear myself saying things to them like, "Do you know who I am? I put Jediism on the map not you guys. I'm out there doing all the media." My ego was fuelled by negativity and defensiveness. It was becoming ugly. It was clearly time to practise what I preach about dealing with negativity and to check my ego. More about this in later chapters, but when you are presented with negativity you have to control your thoughts and not lash out, otherwise you energize or fuel the dark side of the Force and give it more power by becoming a negative Force yourself. You should never let your ego and the darkness of negativity take over and should always send out love and peace when there is hate and conflict.

Today, I reach out with love to all Jedi groups. We all regard *Star Wars* as a sacred text but we are all unique in our approach to the Force. For example, the Temple of the Jedi Order is a Christian Jediist group based on the teachings of Joseph Smith, and other groups have their own specific requirements to join. There are also more open-minded and inclusive groups such as the Jedi Realists, but the Church of Jediism remains the only significant Jedi organization in the world that embraces all religions and belief systems, including atheism. It is also blessed to receive interest from the media and to have a healthy membership. This doesn't mean that bigger is better – simply that the Church of Jediism is a significant spiritual movement.

If I had to define the Church of Jediism I would say it is more a movement offering applied living techniques through philosophical teachings and at its absolute core is the desire to help others. So, for example, one of the church's current Master Jediist faculty trainers, Loyd Auerbach, is Jewish but he can happily support the movement because it does not expect him to renounce his beliefs. In much the same way, Jediist council member Patrick Day Childs is an atheist but he is drawn to the movement because there is no mention of a god but rather that we are all interconnected by the eternal power of love or a Force higher than ourselves and that we live on through our good deeds or our children.

In essence, the Church of Jediism is a modern approach to living with spirituality, purpose, love, compassion and peace and not a religion. We use the word "church" not in the religious sense but in the sense that it is a gathering of like-minded people.

TESTING TIMES

Being human, every Jediist will be tested and there will be times when they lose their way. There will be times when they will betray themselves and others. There will be times when they will doubt, or fail to see the light. There will be times when they hurt someone or make errors, but that is why they are Jediists. They have experienced all this without losing their desire to improve and reunite with the light. Jediism helps you understand that if you can learn and grow from negative experiences, then it is not a failure but a necessary evil, and an opportunity to evolve and form even stronger connections to the Force.

I was certainly tested time and time again during the years I was doing all those media appearances on behalf of the church. The more high profile my church became, the fiercer the criticism and ridicule. It wasn't just making sure my ego didn't take over, it was also making sure I kept my integrity.

To give an example, on one reality TV show I was asked to appear, it soon became clear to me that the producers were manipulating the show. They weren't interested in exploring or promoting Jediism, just ratings. I sensed something wasn't right even before I went on stage for my interview. I was left alone in a waiting room and when I asked to go to the restroom I was escorted there like a prisoner and escorted back to my room afterwards. When I asked for water my "bodyguard" told me they didn't have any and offered me an energy drink or coffee and other toxins and stimulants instead. I declined, as I knew this would increase my chances of getting overstimulated and having one of my meltdowns.

Although my meltdowns were less frequent than when I was in my childhood and teens, frustrating physical and emotional outbursts were still an inexplicable and painful feature of my life. I was always aware that I might lose control at any moment and I know that this unpredictability worried my family and friends greatly. It worried me too but I had learned to live with it. I somehow never lost control in public or injured anyone but myself physically, but there was always that risk – and this show was pushing all my buttons. Before going on stage a researcher, wearing one of those mouthpieces that made her look like a strange security guard, tried to pump me up by getting me to do weird jumping exercises. They clearly wanted me to boost ratings with erratic behaviour. I can't deny I was tempted to fulfil their expectations so I would get a return invitation or more reality show invites and become an overnight celebrity.

Thankfully the Jediist in me clearly sensed what was going on. I was being given an insight into how TV tries to orchestrate reality so the viewer only sees what the producers want to present. Fully aware of that manipulation, when the interviewer started to ask questions that they hoped would act like a trigger, such as telling me that it might come as a shock to me but *Star Wars* wasn't actually real, I kept my cool. I told the presenter that I was real and I was standing right here in front of everyone talking about the power of the universal life Force. The Force was with me because, as the questions leaned further and further towards the derogatory, something totally unexpected and spontaneous happened. Someone from the audience got up, walked towards the stage and asked me how they could join the church. I'm forever grateful to that person and if he is reading this book I hope he will get in touch so I can offer him a long-overdue thank you.

This wasn't an isolated incident. To this day, many interviews typically start with serious misunderstandings about Jediism and inevitable teasing or jokes, but on each occasion I try to turn it around. I sincerely hope that by the end the interviewer and the audience has seen that Jediism isn't a joke or about *Star Wars* fanaticism. It is a peaceful way of life. It is becoming greater than yourself by connecting with the life-changing power of the Force to find your true meaning and help others find theirs.

WHAT IS THE FORCE?

But what exactly is the Force? It really is time now for me to attempt to explain the unexplainable. The basis of Jediism is a mutual respect for the self and the world around you, and positive use of the energy known as the Force to enhance life and achieve goals. The Force is thought of as the cosmic energy that flows in and around all living things, binding us together and tying us with the universe. When the Force flows smoothly, unity is achieved, thus bringing a sense of peace and serenity to all. When the Force flow is interrupted, negativity abounds.

The Force is not some supernatural phenomenon outside you. It is something invisible that lives in your mind and your heart but it can also extend outside of your body and connect you to everyone and everything. Your mind and heart and the Force are not separate but one. Science is even confirming the existence of the Force or consciousness, that part of us that is separate from our bodies and minds and can exist within and all around us.

If you are struggling to get your head around terms such as invisible or cosmic energy, perhaps these examples will help. Sometimes all it takes is a hug from a friend or a piece of good news to raise your energy levels but where does that energy come from? If you've ever seen someone die you will see a spark go out, a little like when a light is switched off, and if you believe in life after death you will feel the spirit of that person live on in your heart and mind. If you've been in love you will know the feeling of euphoric energy that being with your lover gives you. Ancient cultures understood this life energy or the unseen power pulsating through the universe long before we did. In Japan it is called Ki; in China it is called Chi; in India it is Prana. In Christianity it's the Holy Spirit; in yoga the life force is harnessed through the chakra system. In Jediism that unseen energy is called the Force.

Remember what you learned at school. Everything is made up of energy; nothing is truly solid. Even a mountain is constantly moving. Nothing is static or still; it just appears to us that way. It is part of the energy that makes up the universe, the universal energy or the Force. The Force is the core of life and creation. I'm not saying it created life, I'm saying it is what keeps us alive. To illustrate from the world of science: in atoms you have electrons that spin around a nucleus because electromagnetic energy is charging the electrons up. If there was no energy the electrons wouldn't spin, the nucleus wouldn't operate and the atom would implode at an amazing rate. We are made up of billions of atoms and we are full of this blazing energy – and that energy is the Force. It binds our atoms together and creates a structure perfect for operation and survival. In much the same way, the Force is in every living particle and atom that exists in our universe, it is constantly expanding, a powerful energy that flows through us, within us and all around us.

There is no deity, god or higher being involved in Jediism, but there is the Force, that universal energy or consciousness. The Force exists in each one of us and connects us all. It is like a big invisible line of cables interlinking everything. In nature some trees produce sap to destroy ants when they attack but what is amazing is that the trees around them somehow sense this and start producing sap even if there are no ants attacking them. This shows that the trees are in communication with each other somehow. They are tapping into the Force that connects everyone and everything, demonstrating the power of Force sensitivity.

When the Force flows smoothly, unity is achieved, thus bringing a sense of peace and serenity to all.

FORCE SENSITIVITY

When you become aware of the Force within you and connecting you to everyone and everything, you feel this all-consuming and overwhelming energy. You feel intensely alive because you are connecting to the Force. This is called being Force sensitive. A Jediist is judged on being Force sensitive: how positively they can use the Force to guide and inspire them and how fast the energy of the Force can flow through them unblocked by negativity, doubt and fear.

Becoming Force sensitive is about first letting go of the belief sustained by your ego that happiness can be achieved through external sources. A Jediist knows that what he or she seeks comes from within him or herself first. We are all creators, consciously or unconsciously, and if we take responsibility for our thoughts and feelings we create the universe we live in.

Do you know what brings you joy? Many people don't listen to their wisdom within and build a life programmed by family,

YOUR SUPERPOWER

When most people think of a sixth sense or psychic ability they tend to think of intuition, and what we call intuition is a super-sense – a cumulative power of all the other senses: sight, smell, hearing, taste and touch. We are all born with intuition and the ability to unify our senses but most of us aren't using it. Over time, civilization and technology came along to take care of us and we didn't need to rely so much on being alert to our environment to stay alive and away from danger. In short, we got lazy and stopped sensing things around us.

We need to relearn how to notice our intuition, pay attention to it and interpret what it is trying to tell us. We need to rediscover it, train it and develop it each day in much the same way you would build up your physical fitness, or learn a musical instrument or language. Developing your sixth sense is a journey of self-discovery and rediscovery: rediscovering your inborn psychic potential, who you are and what your meaning and purpose are. That is why in the Church of Jediism we pay great attention to the training and development of intuition. It is the superpower of every Jediist.

culture, relationships and job identity, but assuming your identity based on those around you means you forget who you are and the energy flow of the Force is blocked. Inwardly you will feel unfulfilled. Midlife crisis is a classic example of this, when you realize that you've spent your entire life doing what is expected of you rather than what makes you happy. This is when true self-awareness begins and you turn from the outer world to the inner world. You discover your being and what truly brings you joy. Every time you look within for your joy and answers rather than outside of yourself the Force flows faster through you.

Anybody can become Force sensitive. The secret is to truly understand your interconnection with the universe or consciousness; to see yourself as a drop out of an ocean and when you die you return to that ocean. It is also knowing that what your thoughts and heart put out into the universe will return to you. If you walk through life thinking and feeling negative, that is what you will get returned to you because negativity blocks the power of the Force, so always walk with love in your heart and mind.

You will know when you are touched by the Force because you will feel a deep sense of comfort and peace and joy from within. Sometimes you will feel that comfort during the darkest of times. People have these moments all the time and this is the Force at work. People also tap into the Force whenever they pray or feel love and joy or want to help or comfort others. When you "just know" things you are also connecting to the Force. For example, when you sense something has happened before it does. This can also be called intuition or sixth sense or third eye awakening. We see it as bizarre or paranormal but it is not extraordinary. It is simply living in harmony with the Force when your ego (and the fear and doubt it breeds and reliance on external sources of happiness) diminishes and your connection to the Force is clear.

LESSON FOUR: LIVING WITH THE FORCE

Read silently or, better still for the energizing and ritualizing impact, read out loud to yourself the following teaching and then incorporate the practical suggestions into your daily life. Making a commitment to those suggestions is essential otherwise this book is nothing but ideas and words. Too many people get stuck in the "thinking about it" stage but never find the courage or the discipline to do anything about their grand ideas. A Jediist has courage; a Jediist has self-discipline; and a Jediist will also live or embody what he or she believes. If you are to evolve into a Jediist you must move from theory to action as soon as possible. You must both be and do. There is no "I could" or "I might".

The Fourth Teaching on the Force

May the Force, and the love of the universe, and the energy of the light be with you at all times. May your partnership with the Force be strong in all ages and stages of your life, from childhood to maturity.

It is always so simple and natural to explain the concept of the Force – or spiritual energy existing within and around us – to young children, and I urge all those of you who are parents of young children to teach them the ways of Jediism because children are all Jediists at heart. Children see the world as a magical place. They see infinite possibility in things that adults find routine, because their egos and the voices of doubt and fear the ego speaks with are not fully developed until the age of 15. It is sad that as adults we lose this natural and clear connection to the Force. Through the path of Jediism it is possible to return once again to that childlike state of awe and wonder by detaching from external sources of happiness, following our hearts and discovering within ourselves all the wonder we will ever need.

People who follow the Jediist path are often accused of being childlike but we should take that as a compliment, even if it isn't intended to be one, because it means we are connecting to the Force through our inner child. Your inner child is the sensitive, loving, spontaneous and joyful part of your heart and it is where the Force first strives to connect with you. A defining feature of many spiritually advanced souls is that they can often appear childlike – there is a twinkle in their eye, a sense of mischief and fun. Jediism makes its followers and all those who seek it out smile and that is one of the movement's greatest strengths – the way it can make even the most cynical person reconnect with their inner child, feel young at heart again.

Celebrate that connection between your inner child and the Force. Nurture it, because through that connection or partnership you can grow up again, free from negativity, doubt and fear. And as you walk through the ages and stages of your life, from child to adult to Force spirit, never forget that your greatest enemy, or path to the dark side, is not outside you but within you.

Your ego is the natural enemy of the Force, the part of you that doubts and fears and believes you should use the Force for your own advantage rather than the higher or greater good. Knowing your enemy is a powerful way to defeat your enemy, so understand that your ego will always try to use the Force selfishly whereas the true Jediist is selfless. A Jediist knows they are part of something greater than themselves. This isn't to say they don't love themselves. They do, but for a Jediist, loving and helping themselves is the same as loving and helping others because they know we are all connected. Their instinct is to help and serve the greater good. When you are able to sense or feel the loving bonds of interconnection between everyone and everything in the universe you are truly one with the Force, in partnership with the Force and more powerful than it is possible to imagine.

How are you powerful? Let me count the ways.

When you are in partnership with the Force you are serene and wise and measured. You will be able to keep your head when all around you are losing theirs and finding others to blame. You will be able to trust yourself and your heart even when others are doubting you and themselves. You will have patience and understanding, and if others are hurtful or hateful, or criticize you unfairly, you will send them your compassion and not return their hate and injustice with your negativity. You will have humility and share your vision and ideas, but not impose your opinions on others.

When you walk in harmony with the Force you will think about and dream of great things but never allow those thoughts and dreams to consume you, because you know that the Force will only respond if your vision is heartfelt and helps not just yourself but others. You will be able to see both success and failure as teachers and not define yourself by either. You will understand that sometimes people will misunderstand you, however hard you try to bring clarity, and that sometimes you need to let go and accept there are certain things you can't change. You will realize that disappointments and setbacks are opportunities to start afresh with new understanding and hope in your heart.

When you become the Force you will find the courage from within to hold on and not give up when all seems lost. You will not allow others to define you and you will treat all those you encounter, whether they be rich or poor, influential or not, with exactly the same respect, good intention and manners. You won't ever discriminate and will welcome all, regardless of their age, culture and background. And every second of your life you will seek opportunities to help others and live a life of discipline, dedication and deep awareness of and appreciation for the Force alive within and around you.

If you can live in this way, the universe and everything in it will be yours. You will not only be a child of the universe, you will have become the Force and the love and wonder you want to see in the world.

Let us now take a moment to bow our heads and contemplate the blessing of the Force.

A JEDIIST PRAYER FOR THE FORCE

May the Force forever be strong within you and all around you, and may you remember that all power is in your partnership with and awareness of the Force.

When your emotions, or those of others, threaten to overwhelm you, may your partnership with the Force bring you peace and understanding.

When you cannot see a way forward or others misunderstand you, may your connection to the Force bring you knowledge and wisdom.

When there is passion and anger, may the Force bring you serenity and calm.

When there is chaos and fire, may the Force bring you harmony and peace.

When there is death, may your partnership with the Force help you understand that whenever there is love and light there is no death.

Above all, may your sensitivity to the Force guide and inspire your life so that you become a light, a beacon of hope and joy, for others to follow.

How are you powerful? Let me count the ways.

LIVING WITH THE FORCE GUIDELINES

1. Feel the Force

The Force can be tapped into by almost anyone who wants to make the effort to focus and tune into its subtle vibrations. Psychics are no different from you or me: they have simply focused their attention on the Force. One very simple exercise is to focus your attention on the extraordinary in your everyday life. It doesn't have to be dramatic: simple things like the beauty of a sunset, a hunch you had that came true, a coincidence or a dream. Focusing like this will give you a sense of everything and everyone being connected by the hidden energy of the Force.

You can also try this "feel the Force" exercise first thing in the morning and last thing at night when you are lying down comfortably on your back in bed. You can also do this exercise sitting down with your back straight and your hands resting on your thighs.

To begin, take five deep breaths in through the nose and out through the mouth, and as you breathe in imagine that every cell in your body is being filled with energy or light. Then visualize the Force as a bright star emitting light which encircles you, and imagine a milky, bright light seeping into your body. You breathe it in through your nose and breathe it out of your mouth, and as you breathe it out, it circles around your body. Imagine a beacon from your third eye, located in the middle of your forehead, shining into space.

With this feeling of energy and light within and all around you, take five more breaths and this time place your awareness on your heartbeat. Continue to breathe deeply and bring your awareness to your toes and feet. Feel the energy flowing through them as a tingling sensation. Then switch your attention to your hands and arms, and again feel the tingling sensation before moving to your face and feeling the energy sensations there. Then bring your awareness back to your heart and your chest. Finally feel energy moving from your toes up through your entire body and back to your toes again. Keep breathing deeply until you can feel the energy swirling around your body with the heart at the centre.

If you feel any tension in any part of your body, try imagining the energy flowing smoothly through that area to release any blocks to the natural flow.

2. Be still

You are a human being and it is during moments of being rather than doing that it becomes easier to connect with the Force. So for five minutes each day try to simply be. Do nothing but be silent and still. Focus on your breath and find your calm centre.

Keep doing this every day and eventually you will be able to drop outside concerns and become still and in the present. Breathe and be; that is all you need to do. If you find that too challenging, play some relaxing music. The aim is to let go of the mental chatter. You do this naturally when you are absorbed in a task you love, such as writing, drawing, driving or exercising. You lose sense of time as you are immersed, and in this expansive open-minded state you can connect to the Force. This is the state when you let go and allow the universe to take you where you need to be. Many people fight this. They believe it takes effort to succeed and dreamers are timewasters, but the opposite is true. Dreamers are the ones with the power to change the world because in moments of heightened awareness or absorption you are connecting to the Force and seeing possibilities, potentials and connections between everyone and everything.

Above all, in moments of stillness you discover that what you seek is within. All your life people have told you to follow your heart but you never really thought that was true – but it is. You don't have to hit rock bottom or experience pain and heartache to discover depth within yourself and the light that will connect you to the Force. You can discover it in moments of silence and stillness when you hear that voice from within.

3. Find your forward motion

Have you watched the sense of purpose a child has when they are learning to walk? It is amazing. Why can't you have that purpose in your daily life? There are many ways to find your purpose but the main ways are creating or doing something that helps or inspires others in some way, because whenever you help others you are consciously or unconsciously one with the Force. Forget about competing and focus on creating.

Another way to raise your vibration is to care for another person or thing; to forget about getting and focus on giving in terms of your time, your smile, your money, your kind words and so on. You can become the Force when you discover within yourself the courage you never thought you had to face challenge, or to deal with pain or the negative opinions of others. Not giving up on your dreams or letting other people trample on your dreams are powerful ways to connect you to the Force.

4. Feel the sun

The best way to do this exercise is at sunrise or sunset when the sun isn't too strong. Never ever stare directly at the sun, even during sunrise and sunset, because it can cause serious damage to your eyes. For this exercise avert your eyes from the sun, or close them, and place your face in the direction of the sun rising or setting so you can feel its warm rays on your face and body. In this way you are drinking in the energy of the Force as the sun gives life to this planet and is the main component of the living life Force. Allowing the rays of the sun to touch your face can bring an awareness of connectivity with everyone and everything in the universe.

5. See what is hidden

This exercise is designed to awaken your sensitivity to the Force. It sounds odd but I'm going to ask you to stare at a plant. It is a hard exercise and will need practice, so don't be discouraged if you don't see immediate results.

You need to find a young plant and study it in detail. Look at its colour, shape and texture, and then let this thought fill your mind: this plant will one day become a bigger plant. Now picture in your mind that bigger plant. See what it will become. If you do this exercise for a few days you may begin to see that plant in your mind's eye and you may even see a mist or cloud surrounding it. It isn't staring at the plant that has triggered this image but your understanding that every living being is surrounded by the Force and has a greater destiny or higher potential in store for it.

6. Practise Force sensitive techniques daily

The Force can help you transform your life for the better. It wants to help you solve your issues and reach your full potential, if only you will let it. Here are some force techniques you can use daily, or as and when needed, to help you realize your higher potential. All of them will boost your energy and confidence and/or help you release tension and find inner peace and by so doing help you connect to the Force.

- Imagine you are close to death and angry at yourself right now for not living life to the full. The energy boost you get from this reminds you how precious time is and that you are here for a reason.

- Learn to consider your thoughts carefully, and engaging the energy of joy will strengthen your connection to the Force. Perhaps the simplest way to give yourself an energy boost and feel the Force is to focus your attention on what you have to be grateful for. There is power in an attitude of gratitude.

- Aim to focus your thoughts on what you want to materialize in your life. Many of us make the mistake of focusing on what we don't want to happen in our lives and because thoughts create our reality that is what we get. For example, if you are worried about not having enough money, you won't have enough money. Start thinking about ways to earn or make money instead and you will draw opportunities your way.

- Essential oils can bring healing and feelings of energy, possibility and connection. I recommend using frankincense and sandalwood.

- If you are feeling nervous or anxious, take a breath and then for the next breath make it bigger and continue until you are panting. It's a simple technique but it really can release tension and raise your energy vibration.

- Another exercise I often recommend for those times when you feel anxious is to do the "Princess Leia" or "Han Solo" pose. Pull your shoulders back and stand with your hands on your hips. This pose induces feelings of personal power and self-worth.

Becoming Force sensitive through mindfulness, meditation, yoga, and diet will also help you discover your full potential, and these important techniques will be discussed later in the book. Developing these techniques lays the foundation stone for developing superpowers – such as sensing things before they happen, moving objects with the power of thought and reading minds – through your connection to the Force. All this may sound like science fiction but there is very credible research to suggest that the human mind is capable of the most remarkable feats and that our sixth sense is just like all our other senses but we have been taught to fear and doubt it by religion and society. The Church of Jediism offers training in psychic development, should you so choose, as it believes in the infinite possibilities of the human mind. The adventure continues...

I AM A JEDIIST

Legendary parapsychologist, Loyd Auerbach, talks about what the Force means to him (https://en.wikipedia.org/wiki/Loyd_Auerbach). Loyd is a Jediist Master trainer on the Church of Jediism faculty.

I am a parapsychologist. We study extrasensory perception (information abilities), psychokinesis (mind interacting with matter and energy) and survival of bodily death (including apparitions and reincarnation) – together called psi phenomena – all of which have examples in *Star Wars* (especially the Expanded Universe, the original fictional material licensed by Lucasfilm). Since the field's start in the late 1800s, we've learned much about patterns of the experiences, personality and other human variables of those experiencing or using psi abilities, and even some apparent environmental connections, including to the Earth's geomagnetic field.

What we do not have a real handle on is how information might transfer over vast distances instantly, from the future, or even from the past. We do not know what physical mechanism allows our minds to seemingly move objects, heal people or interact with computers and other electronics. And we certainly do not know what an apparition (ghost) is made of, contrary to what so many paranormal TV shows like to say.

However, we do have various models we're looking at, and researchers in my field look to fields of physical science for hints at what might be going on, and for new theories and models of the physical universe and the brain that could relate and help us form our own theories and models. That said, the focus of such theorizing often centres on the question of what consciousness is, a question which is of great debate even among physical scientists (not to mention those in the metaphysical and religious worlds).

In parapsychology so many of the experiences people have and the abilities they display show an interconnectedness of consciousness to the physical world, to each other, to other living things and through time itself. Where the "energy" to do any of this comes from is still speculative; however, it's as likely as not that this is the wrong way to think about what's going on, that instead we may be tapping into something that allows connections over distances and time similar to what happens with quantum entanglement (though at a much greater size, of course).

This concept of the Force was hardly new with George Lucas. The idea of a unified field throughout the universe has come to us in science from Albert Einstein. Physicists today continue to search for such a "force" that ties all other energy forms and matter in the universe together. Such an idea has also existed in various schools of mysticism in cultures around the world.

The idea that people can tap into the universal life force is also not new, but the *Star Wars* saga perhaps brought it to life in a way people all over the world could relate to.

What more than a couple of the models put forward to explain psi in its myriad forms is that human consciousness taps into a universal field to grab information, transfer information to others, move objects, and so on. This is even one explanation given to explain seeming past life memories, and certainly hauntings where the witnesses tap into something and replay past events in their perceptions. Apparitions seem to be pure consciousness, still capable of connecting with the minds of the living, and perhaps connecting with such a universal field to support their very existence (that last is my own speculation).

At least one of my colleagues has speculated the field is the zero point energy field. One thing is clear: we are tapping into something that connects us all. As a metaphor for such a field, the Force allows us to craft models that hopefully can one day lead to actual understanding and development of genuine psychic powers.

Allow the universal life Force to flow through you unrestricted by fear and you will feel the greatest joy and see the greatest wonder you have ever seen.

Daniel M. Jones

Chapter
FIVE

Emotional Control and Anger Management

Patience you must have, my young Padawan.

Popularly ascribed to Yoda, *Star Wars Episode V: The Empire Strikes Back*

Once
you begin to tap into the living life Force – the loving glue that binds everyone and everything together – you become limitless potential and experience the most indescribable joy. However, just as night always follows day, you can't have joy without sadness, or light without the dark side of the Force. Jediism does not deny the existence of the dark side. Instead it recognizes and accepts that, for reasons we can't understand, the dark side both within and around us is a reality we need to face with courage. It offers applied living techniques to help us navigate our way through the storm and grow wiser in the process.

I deliberately avoided focusing on the dark side of the Force until this point in the book because in my own life I have found that the best way to manage the dark side is not to give it the spotlight. That just fuels or feeds negativity and makes it grow stronger. However, a wise Jediist must be aware that darkness exists and be able to recognize it when it strikes so he or she can learn from it and then move forward with greater self-awareness. The dark side thrives on attention and addiction. Starve it of both and it will have no power over you. This profound life lesson was something I had to learn the hard way.

THE GROCERY EMPIRE STRIKES BACK

In 2009 I found myself making national newspaper headlines again – but this time for all the wrong reasons. Here's the *Guardian* feature headline:

"Jedi religion founder accuses Tesco of discrimination over rules on hoods"

Pretty attention-grabbing! Things got worse with the rest of the feature.

"Tesco has been accused of religious discrimination after the company ordered the founder of a Jedi religion to remove his hood or leave a branch of the supermarket in North Wales."

Yes, I really did make an official complaint. Not only did that complaint end up in the *Guardian* newspaper and other British national newspapers, it went right up to Fox and CNN TV news as well. After the 2008 *Star* feature and the explosion of interest that followed, things had finally started to settle down for Jediism in terms of media interest but suddenly I was back in the intense glare of the spotlight.

The *Guardian* feature went on to describe the unsavoury incident with great relish, accompanied by pictures of me in my hood looking particularly defiant, mean and moody. Looking at those pictures now, I'd probably ask myself to leave the supermarket.

"Daniel Jones, founder of the religion inspired by the Star Wars *films, says he was humiliated and victimized for his beliefs following the incident at a Tesco store in Bangor. The 23-year-old, who founded the International Church of Jediism, which has 500,000 followers worldwide, was told the hood flouted store rules."*

Yes, those were my words. I said I was "humiliated and victimized" because while out doing some grocery shopping and minding my own business I was told to remove my hood or leave the store. I looked around me and saw a man wearing a hat and a woman wearing a scarf and another wearing a burkha. I lost the plot. At the time it felt like stereotyping because I was a young male with a hoodie and piercings. I was puffed up with anger and hurt pride, and before I knew it things had spiralled out of control. Tesco defended its policy and what was ironic was that they defended it by referencing their obvious fondness for *Star Wars*. I can see all that irony now but at the time all I saw was my anger.

"But the grocery empire struck back, claiming that the three best-known Jedi Knights in the Star Wars *movies – Yoda, Obi-Wan Kenobi and Luke Skywalker – all appeared in public without their hoods. Jones, from Holyhead, who is known by the Jedi name Morda Hehol, said his religion dictated that he should wear the hood in public places and is considering legal action against the chain. 'It states in our Jedi doctrine that I can wear headwear. It just covers the back of my head,' he said. 'You have a choice of wearing headwear in your home or at work but you have to wear a cover for your head when you are in public.'"*

Yes, in the early days of Jediism I did give guidelines about clothing, and one of them strongly recommended wearing a hood in public to cover the back of the head.

At the time I felt that it was important for my followers to have a sense of collective identity and that is why I made the recommendations. Today there are no such clothing requirements as I've realized that placing emphasis on external or material things in this way simply isn't the way of the Jediist because what a Jediist seeks can only be found within. Back in 2009, however, the incident felt like an attack on me and my religious beliefs.

"'They said: "Take it off", and I said: "No, it's part of my religion. It's part of my religious right." I gave them a Jedi church business card. They weren't listening to me and were rude. They had three people around me. It was intimidating.' Jones, who has made an official complaint to Tesco, is considering a boycott of the store and is seeking legal advice."

Yes, I did consult with my lawyers and waste a lot of my time, money and energy considering a lawsuit over something so trivial. It was just a simple misunderstanding I could easily have defused but I let my ego and the dark side take over. Reading this feature now I can see that Tesco weren't the evil and prejudiced controllers I thought they were and were in fact fairly light-hearted in their approach to me. Here was their final word on the matter.

"Tesco said: 'He hasn't been banned. Jedis are very welcome to shop in our stores although we would ask them to remove their hoods. Obi-Wan Kenobi, Yoda and Luke Skywalker all

appeared hoodless without ever going over to the Dark Side and we are only aware of the Emperor as one who never removed his hood. If Jedi walk around our stores with their hoods on, they'll miss lots of special offers.'"

A week or so after the incident my anger settled down and I took a good long hard look at myself. I realized I had let the dark side take over. As a Jediist I should have found a way to defuse the situation with harmony and peace. I wasn't doing my religion any favours. I could have stated my case in a calm and peaceful manner and then left the store. Instead, I lost my temper and confirmed their suspicions about young men in hoods being troublemakers. I let myself and my church down.

The incident was unsavoury, but with the benefit of hindsight I can now see that this was the Force at work too. I stepped over to the dark side and learned a lot about myself and my anger issues in the process and also what was and was not essential for Jediism (hoods certainly aren't). The Force rewarded my desire to learn from an unpleasant experience with the evolution of Jediism, because much to my surprise the incident actually drew even more attention and followers to my church!

DANCING IN THE DARK

Jediism, as I explained earlier, acknowledges the existence of the dark side of the Force. It does not waste too much time and energy trying to understand why evil and injustice exist, because it accepts that we are unlikely ever to fully understand the big "whys" of the universe. It's better to place our mental energy into finding inner peace and making the world a better place.

Personally, I think our lives are a bit like the underside of a tapestry, all knots and loose ends but then if you turn over the tapestry you see the beautiful image on the other side. Perhaps the bigger picture where everything makes perfect sense is what we will see when we die and our spiritual essence becomes one with the Force. It is impossible to know for sure. All that really matters in Jediism is what you are doing with the precious gift of your life right now.

Jediism is therefore not so much concerned with the nature of evil and negativity as how to work through the darkness. We see pain and suffering as unavoidable parts of our evolution we need to face with courage, since more often than not encountering the dark side triggers spiritual growth and awakens our greater potential. I'll give another example of working through negativity from my own life. It's different from the Tesco incident because that was an internal problem for me. It taught me that I had anger and ego issues and I was placing importance on things that really didn't matter. This incident was about negativity manifesting outside of me – in this instance through someone in my life.

When someone has been your friend from childhood – and remember, I didn't have many friends when I was growing up due to my condition – you relax around them. You trust them but when that trust is betrayed it is unbearably painful. To cut a long story short, someone I thought was my close friend lied to and stole from me. When I found out what he had done it was like a knife went into my heart. I felt betrayed, hurt, angry, sad, confused, and every other emotion.

Looking back, there were times when I was growing up when I got alarm bells about this guy but because he was my best friend, and I had known him forever, I ignored them. For example, I would often hear him being flexible with the truth with friends and family, or he would suddenly fall off the radar for months without explanation and then return as if nothing had happened. I forgave him each time because he was my friend and that's what friends do. All the while, though, my instinct was telling me something was off, but I refused to listen to my intuition, which is a guaranteed way for a Jediist to lose his or her way.

I'm very direct so I decided to confront my friend about what had happened. He explained how tough things had been for him and to his credit he apologized and asked how to make amends. I accepted his apology and told him it wasn't about the money and there was no need to pay me back. It was about him betraying our friendship and how much that hurt me. We have moved forward now and I wish him well but I learned something very important from this painful experience. I learned to trust no one.

I'm sure you were surprised by my last statement, as Jediism preaches unconditional love and always seeing the best in people. That is certainly what is recommended, but if you put too much trust in someone you open yourself up to exploitation.

Of course, you can trust and hope for the best in others but at the same time you must remember every human being is vulnerable to the dark side of the Force. Indeed, facing the dark side is essential because it is through our encounters with it that we learn and evolve.

Another profound lesson I learned is always to trust my instinct about people. My friend letting me down also helped me deal better with friendships and relationships. I am grateful to him because he taught me not to need or rely on other people for a sense of meaning and fulfilment, or to assume that someone who you think loves you will always have your best interests at heart. Buddha said that the person who loves ten people has ten problems but the person who loves no one has no problems. Again this doesn't mean you should not love other people, it means you should not need them or rely on them to make you happy. The only person in life you can rely on is yourself, and even then you will let yourself down from time to time. I'm being realistic here and aware that we are all works in progress. The sooner we all find inner peace and self-love the happier and more fulfilled we will be.

EMOTIONAL MANAGEMENT

Dancing with the dark side of the Force – feeling negative emotions such as hate, jealousy, fear, guilt and anger – is all part of human experience. There is nothing wrong with feeling difficult emotions. Emotions in themselves are not negative or bad; they are necessary for us to grow and develop. It is only when we act on negative emotions that they become bad, and the way to prevent that happening is to learn how to manage our emotions.

Jediism encourages you to feel the full range of emotions instead of questioning and denying them. You may find it uncomfortable to acknowledge difficult emotions, but feelings that are painful can alert you to an area of discomfort in your life. Emotions that are suppressed or denied cause even greater stress because you are not allowing yourself to feel what is true for you. Emotions are messages from the Force and if they are not worked through, this will cause great tension.

Indeed, emotions are the only real way you have to show what matters to you and what doesn't. Negative emotions signal the need for some kind of change in our lives, be that from within or in your daily life. We all have our own pressure points and for me that is especially the case as I have Asperger's. My pressure point is anger.

Asperger's and anger go hand in hand. I have had extensive anger management therapy and learned a great deal about myself and how my brain works as a result. I have learned that I have an issue with communication and coping with frustration. This was intensified when, because my Asperger's was undiagnosed, I was forced into mainstream education that had no understanding of how to treat people with my condition. I had no specialist school training where I could learn how to manage my anger and develop social skills. Instead I found ways to teach myself. I watched hours and hours of video footage of people I admired and studied how they spoke to increase my vocabulary and knowledge basis. What I was trying to do was to understand how people communicate effectively and manage their emotions.

For many people with Asperger's, managing anger successfully and positively is the Holy Grail, as if we can do that we can blend in. In my childhood and teens I would often break my own fingers and smash my toes in fits of uncontrollable rage when things didn't go my way. The trigger would be anything that took me away from my normal routine, even something as subtle as a change in temperature or a new or certain smell (I can't be anywhere near the smell of garlic or onions). To this day routine is very important for me. I can have my day planned, and I'm fine if everything goes according to plan, but if one thing is out of order or doesn't follow a pattern, then I can have a meltdown.

During my teens I couldn't control my meltdowns. I would also get the urge to pull out my hair. It wasn't until I reached the age of 26 that I was tested for Asperger's on the advice of a friend, and discovered that I do indeed have a medical condition. I also realized that Jediism was in many ways my attempt to train my emotions so I could function normally in society. If I had a meltdown I used Jediism-inspired applied living techniques to guide me to a place of peace and calm, and if I had a fit of anger or an anxious moment I could again use those techniques to self-soothe with the minimum of disruption. For example, I don't freak out in a sandwich shop anymore if they have run out of the brown bread I prefer. I have learned to enter any situation with options so if my first choice doesn't work out I have at least two backups. In the case of sandwiches with brown bread I ask for brown rolls if they have run out or wholemeal muffins and so on.

Emotions in themselves are not negative or bad; they are necessary for us to grow and develop.

Again, I feel my Asperger's has been a blessing because I have learned how to deal with it and use that knowledge to help other people with Asperger's and people in general. Today I mentor people who have Asperger's via my popular Aspie World YouTube channel. I have developed a framework to help me manage my emotions and I share it with my Aspie followers. That framework is Jediism-inspired because Jediism doesn't just help me navigate my way through life with Asperger's, it also helps everyone work through and manage their negative emotions.

WORKING THROUGH THE DARK SIDE

The Force has a light and a dark side. Love, joy, harmony, peace and hope are the energetic power of the light side whereas the dark side of the Force draws its power from negative emotions such as jealousy, anger, fear and hate. The dark side can be very seductive and deceptive as it promises you the fantasy of unlimited power and can disguise itself in falsehoods and the pretence of goodness or what is best for you. It seduces you by making you think that your interests are more important than the natural order or what is for the greater good – as is the case for Anakin in *Revenge of the Sith* when he attempts to cheat death. However, any action that opposes the natural order will end in confusion and pain.

The dark side of the Force lives within us and around us, and throughout our lives we will encounter it because light cannot exist without darkness. The key is to work through the darkness, and learn and grow from it rather than let the experience drain and destroy love and joy from you. You should not ever feel disappointed with yourself if you have negative feelings, such as anger or sadness. You are human and this is part of the experience – and just because you feel a negative emotion does not mean you have to act on it. A Jediist learns how to manage and control their emotions. When they notice that their emotions are tempting them to the dark side and hurting them in the process, they remind themselves that they are in charge of their emotions and not the other way round. They know that nothing can make you feel angry, sad, guilty or scared unless you allow it to.

When the dark side manifests externally in other people or in difficult situations, Jediism teaches us to observe the situation and learn from it. What is going on in your life that is attracting this person or situation to you? For example, when my friend betrayed me, the Force was teaching me to pay attention to my gut instinct about people as there had been warning signs. When the supermarket wanted to exclude me for wearing a hood, the Force was urging me to find a way to handle my anger. There is always something to learn from every negative situation.

Bear in mind too that the people in your life can reflect aspects of yourself to a certain extent. If you encounter someone who doesn't treat you with respect, see that as a message from the Force to work on your self-esteem. If someone truly hurts you, the best and highest response is not to return hate with hate, otherwise you become the monster you are fighting. Recognize that aspect within yourself but don't act on it. Love the fact that you have no negative thoughts about this person and that you aren't feeding the dark side of the Force with revenge. Leave that person to understand and work through their own pain, and continue the journey of your own life. Trust that the laws of the universe will ensure that somewhere and somehow that person will meet justice.

In essence, the response of a Jediist to negative emotions and situations is to face them with courage and calm, and then choose to move on. Nothing disarms and weakens the dark side more than your neutrality towards it. Holding a grudge is like holding a piece of hot coal, waiting to throw it at the person you are angry with. You are the one who gets hurt. The more you engage with negativity the more it will evolve. Don't engage. Release and let go.

Nothing disarms and weakens the dark side more than your neutrality towards it.

LESSON FIVE: LIVING WITH FEELING

Read silently or, better still for the energizing and ritualizing impact, read out loud to yourself the following teaching and then incorporate the practical suggestions into your daily life. Making a commitment to those suggestions is essential otherwise this book is nothing but ideas and words. Too many people get stuck in the "thinking about it" stage but never find the courage or the discipline to do anything about their grand ideas. A Jediist has courage; a Jediist has self-discipline; and a Jediist will also live or embody what he or she believes. If you are to evolve into a Jediist you must move from theory to action as soon as possible. You must both be and do. There is no "I could" or "I might".

The Fifth Teaching on the Force

It is a blessing to have your absolute attention. May what you read or hear now help you to manage your emotions so that the dark side of the Force has no power over you. May what you read here help you grow stronger each time you encounter the dark side.

When the dark side is pulling you towards it with feelings of anger, hate and fear, accept what you are feeling and take responsibility for it even if it is painful. Never deny feelings of sadness or anger, or blame others for them. Never think that because you feel anger you are an angry person, or because you feel sad you are a sad person. You are not your emotions. You are feeling the dark side of the Force within you for a reason, so feel it. If you feel sad, cry. Tears are not a sign of weakness but a sign of strength. If you feel angry, release that anger in a safe way. Scream out loud if you have to. Never deny your feelings. Remind yourself that you always have a choice. If you feel anger or hate you do not have to act on that anger or hate. You can find ways to manage it and channel it into something positive. Managing your feelings in this way can only enrich your life. Feeling something is what humans are born to do.

There will, of course, be times in the lives of all Jediist when they must journey through the most unbearable pain but these are the times when the Force is closer to them than ever. You may feel abandoned and alone but you are not. The Force is calling out to you through your pain to awaken spiritually and grow. Think of grief, loss, sorrow and pain as the darkness before the dawn.

You may wonder during times of darkness why you are experiencing such pain. It will feel unfair and unjust especially if you have been living a life of love and gratitude. You may wonder why the universe is sending darkness your way. This takes us to the eternal question: "Why do bad things happen to good people?" There is no answer, and a Jediist should not try to answer but simply accept that sometimes, as in the case of Obi-Wan dying, there is a bigger picture, a higher reason for the suffering of good people

Life is very much like school – a spiritual school. We are spiritual beings in human form, and because we are in human form we are susceptible to negative human feelings. However, our task is to overcome those barriers, learn from our experiences – even negative ones – and grow spiritually. Spiritual growth occurs when we finally come to a point when we understand that our essence is eternal pure consciousness that flows within and around us. We have infinite potential and when we shed our human form we will return to that pure consciousness – the Force – either strengthened or weakened by our time on Earth. If we have followed the light and become enlightened, we strengthen the power of the Force, but the opposite is true if we allowed negativity to get the upper hand.

Becoming part of the Force means accepting that sometimes the journey of your life will involve pain and hardship, and you need to learn to see pain as something that sets you free, helps you shed old skins so you can be transformed. A pearl is exquisite and precious but we must not forget that it has been created by an injured life. May you one day feel gratitude for the pain you have walked through.

The path of instant gratification is the one that the great majority of us take, but a Jediist will always take the path less travelled, because they understand that life isn't meant to be easy. They can learn and grow from overcoming challenges, obstacles and suffering. With this awareness and clear vision they understand that fulfilment in life can only be achieved with an attitude of discipline, patience and hard work. They don't avoid challenges and are under no illusion that their lives will always be blissful and problem-free. Indeed a life without problems would be a very empty, superficial and meaningless life as the reason for our existence is to learn and grow, and being in a state of constant bliss would mean there was no need to learn and grow anymore. This is not to say that a Jediist doesn't strive for happiness and harmony at all times. They most certainly do, but they strive for it knowing that happiness and harmony are spiritual gifts and ideals rather than a permanent destination.

Hold this prayer close to your heart at all times.

A JEDIIST PRAYER FOR THE LIGHT

May you always be open and kind, and see the light and the potential for goodness and greatness in everyone and everything you encounter.

May you also proceed through your life with calm and

caution and forever be alert to the potential for darkness to manifest within yourself and in others.

May you accept that the dark side exists but refuse to allow it to consume you.

May you always choose the light, and walk in peace, calm and harmony with the Force.

May you become a light to inspire others because you have encountered the darkness and so grown in self-awareness and strengthened your connection with the Force.

May you never stop asking why there is darkness in the world because every time you ask why, you reveal the empathy and love in your heart. Wherever there is empathy and love there is light.

Take a moment of reflection now to rejoice in and be thankful your emotions. Feelings, even ones that are unwelcome, are a blessing and the source of all creativity, progress, enlightenment, transformation and love. Feel the Force flow clearly through you.

EMOTIONAL LIVING GUIDELINES

1. Take the path less travelled

I highly recommend a book called *The Road Less Travelled* by M. Scott Peck. It does have a Christian bias (which I don't endorse as Jediism welcomes all faiths and beliefs, including atheism), but it is a masterful description of what attributes it takes to make a fulfilled human being. The book discusses the importance of discipline, which is essential for mental, emotional and spiritual health. The elements of discipline which create fulfilment include the ability to delay gratification, accepting responsibility for yourself and your actions, dedicating your life to truth in words and actions, and balancing your own needs with those of others.

Peck then goes on to discuss the ultimate feeling, which is love, and how our notions about it are often incorrect. We don't fall in love and love is not something that happens to us. Love is an action and a conscious decision and it is what links us to "a force other than our conscious will" and this force nurtures spiritual growth in us all. The book is a heart-opening read and although Mr Peck passed away in 2005 I sense the Force was strong with him and remains strong to this day.

2. Find your calm centre

Before you can even start working through your emotions you must first get to a calm place or find your calm centre. That isn't as easy as it sounds as today many of us feel overwhelmed. If this is the case for you, find some time each day to go somewhere quiet, or better still where you can be completely alone in the dark. Once there, close your eyes and take some deep breaths, inhaling through your nose and exhaling through your mouth.

3. Energy tapping

Energy tapping or emotional freedom technique (EFT) is a form of emotional release that you may want to research and experiment with. I highly recommend it. Tapping is a soothing form of touch based on the ancient idea from Chinese medicine of there being a flow of vital energy (Chi or Qi) along meridian pathways in our body. Tapping points are found on these meridians and it seems that tapping them activates our body's innate self-healing intelligence. As exciting and simple as this sounds, it is important to point out that it does not work for everyone but those who do find it helpful swear by it. As with everything in life the only way to find out if it can help you is to try it out for yourself.

EMOTIONAL FREEDOM TECHNIQUE

Emotional freedom technique (EFT) is a form of counselling and therapy that utilizes a number of therapies from alternative medicine derived from the ancient Chinese philosophy or Chi (life force which flows through the body), including acupuncture, energy medicine and acupressure. *The EFT Handbook* by Gary Craig popularized the therapy.

To date there have been no credible research studies but advocates believe it can treat many physical and emotional disturbances and once you know the basic principles and tapping points on the body it can be self-administered. During an EFT session a person will typically focus on a specific physical and/or emotional issue while tapping on related energy points on the body.

4. Find ways to manage specific emotions

Sometimes you won't understand why you feel a certain way but on other occasions you will be able to identify clearly the emotion that you are feeling. The first step to managing your emotions is to understand that just because you feel something does not mean it defines you. For example, if you feel anger this means anger is passing through you and not that you are an angry person. The next step is to understand that because you are not your emotions you can choose how to manage them. You can take positive action depending on the emotion you are feeling:

Sadness and disappointment:

- Acknowledge and release those feelings and have a good cry. Tears are very healing. Showing your emotions is a sign of honesty and strength not weakness.
- Comfort yourself with kindness and accept help from others.
- See what you can learn from the experience and how it can help you make better decisions in the future.
- If someone hurts you, don't forget but do forgive them and move forward.
- If the criticism they give is valid be grateful, as sometimes we do need to be told where we are losing our way. If, however, someone is extremely unfair or hurtful again send them your gratitude because they are showing you a path of negativity that you don't want to follow.

Guilt:

- Acknowledge that your life is being ruled by "should"s and "ought"s and think about what whether these values are yours or those of others.
- Learn from your mistakes and if you have hurt someone make amends.
- Surround yourself with people who respect and value you for who you are and not what you do.
- Focus on your strengths not weaknesses.

Anger:

- Understand what has the potential to trigger episodes of anger and make a plan to counteract that.
- Practise stress management techniques (more about that in Chapter 7).
- Find an activity that releases pent-up tension or a way to channel your anger in a positive way.
- If you lose your cool, reflect on the situation and how you will act differently next time.
- Think about what is worth getting angry about and what isn't.

Fear:

- Practise correct breathing and stress management techniques (Chapter 7).
- Talk to yourself in a calm and constructive and positive way.
- Imagine yourself being calm and bring that image to mind.

- Mentally prepare yourself before going into stressful situations. See yourself navigating them with ease.

Jealousy and envy
- Think of these emotions as information telling you what you really want for yourself. Add this to your personal goals. If your goals are achievable, be prepared to work hard towards them. If they are unrealistic, modify them in some way.
- Always keep a sense of what you value and what your goals are.

Apathy
- Keep mentally and physically active and healthy (see Chapter 8).
- Visit new places, meet new people and learn and do new things.
- See beauty in the everyday.

Loving too much
- If you think your life can't be complete without someone else then you condemn yourself to a life of dependence on the whims of others. You are a reed blown in the wind. A Jediist is content both in their own company and in the company of others. They love being with people but do not need others to complete them, despite the messages Hollywood movies give us.

- If you can't feel content in your own company you will never feel fulfilled in the company of others. Enjoy the company of others but don't put them on pedestals and never change who you are inside for another person or have just one key relationship. Change because it feels right for you and nurture several strong relationships. If you do start a special relationship don't neglect the other people who care about you. Above all, value the importance of personal space so you never run the risk of getting lost in others.

Throughout the process of managing your emotions you should always try to seek the positive potential in every situation. However, you should also remember that there is both a light and a dark side to the Force and nothing in life is ever wholly good or bad. Sometimes for reasons we simply can't understand it is good to feel bad because feeling bad is a powerful incentive for personal transformation.

5. Choose your friends wisely

It is often said that we are the sum of the five people we feel closest to, so choose your friends wisely. Think about those five people and what they say about your character and your values. Do they reflect who you are? If they don't, then you need to think about who you are welcoming into your life and begin to set boundaries. Remember too that people, however much you trust them, always have the potential to hurt you, so never rely too much on others. The only person you should rely on is yourself – and even then you may find that you let yourself down from time to time but that is fine as we are humans. There is no such thing as perfection as perfection is a static lifeless state whereas the Force is a constant swirl of life, energy and infinite potential for growth.

Don't give others the power to control your emotions or let them drag you into their dramas. Retain your boundaries and be your own source of comfort, joy and inspiration. When welcoming people into your life one trick that works for me is to pay more attention to what they do rather than what they say. As Qui-Gon Jinn says in *The Phantom Menace*, "The ability to speak does not make you intelligent" and eloquence, charm and charisma do not make a person trustworthy. Always look beneath the surface and remember that what people present to the world is just the tip of an iceberg.

I AM A JEDIIST

Jo Angel (www.joangel.co.uk) is a qualified life coach, intuitive, EFT and NLP (Neuro Linguistic Programming) practitioner with over 20 years of professional experience helping people to reach their full potential. She is a Jediist Master trainer for the Church of Jediism. Here she talks about how connecting to the Force has helped her manage emotional pain and emerge wiser, stronger and empowered.

I have been using the "Force" for over 20 years in life and my career, but it wasn't until I was introduced to *Star Wars* a few years ago, that it all connected with me and I was amazed how a film had been using this as a concept for all this time. I was only seven years old when I first went to see the film and was unaware until recently of its powerful message.

The "force of being a Jediist" is that of love, and spiritual connection. It is an instinctive knowing of love, peace and the right thing to do. But what do we do when we feel that we cannot live up to these ideal expectations at certain times in our lives?

Emotional pain is an example that we can use. I myself have been through many challenges, and faced extreme emotional pain many times over. I am one of many I know, but I am writing this from a real perspective and not just a third-party overview. I also know that anger, frustration, depression, low self-esteem/confidence, addictions and fear, to name but a few, are what we must face and deal with in our real everyday human lives. So how do we cope?

Well, firstly we must accept and acknowledge these feelings, and respect that they are trying to teach us something valuable. What do we need to move away from? What is happening past, present or future that is so bad for us that we are recognizing this shift in our mind, body and spirit?

Denial, blame or anger towards another person is not the way forward in trying to heal. This is also the equivalent of holding onto a burning piece of wood, and expecting someone else to feel the pain. It is pointless. So, we must keep moving and work through the quagmire of emotions until we find what changes are needed. You must remember that throughout this very uncomfortable journey, you will still be the only one holding the power. Nobody else but you. This is what we often forget.

Everything in this life is temporary and nothing stays the same. Own your feelings. Embrace them and allow them to be your guide. Your emotions and feelings change with time, but your teachings will continue until you listen. I am not saying this is easy as I know from first-hand experience, but I am telling you that it is possible as I have seen this time and time again. Breakdowns are often "breakthroughs" if you don't try to cover them over with a huge "mental blanket". It is also okay to be angry, to express, to show emotions as it takes time and dedication for some to work on developing their "emotional intelligence" and how to work with it for your higher good, and not against it.

It is never okay, though, to be cruel. There is no excuse, ever, for harming another based on your emotions. This is your responsibility to seek the help and support needed so that your fearful emotions do not go on to destroy another's life.

Love and fear are very closely linked, in my opinion. You can love something so much, but experience fear of losing it at the same time. It is love that will allow it to stay, not fear. And "Fear of our emotions is what will keep us in fear of our emotions"!

Trust, faith and love are your only way out, and within. Life can hit us like an erupting volcano at times, and you never know when or if you will ever recover. That strength really is within each of us and that is your power. Your force will be your guide always.

The most painful lessons are the ones we need to learn the most from. When we learn to appreciate those painful lessons we have grown in emotional wisdom and spiritual power. We have found inner peace. We have become one with the Force.

Daniel M. Jones

Chapter
SIX

Self-Defence and Martial Arts

The belonging you seek is not behind you. It is ahead.

Maz, *Star Wars Episode VII: The Force Awakens*

A Jediist walks with an open mind and an open heart in harmony with the swirling energy and potential of the living life Force. They are aware of the seductive and deceptive potential of the dark side but make a choice to focus their intentions on the light side. Although the darkness offers instant gratification and external rewards, Jediists know the price is emptiness and pain inside. The light side of the Force is the only place to find true meaning but that sense of wholeness must come from within.

The moment when a Jediist learns that true power comes from within and can't be found outside him or herself is the most powerful turning point for a Jediist; the defining moment of their lives. Armed with inner strength and self-awareness a Jediist commands respect from everyone they encounter and can bring light into the world simply by being him or herself and not by doing.

Although my early research had taught me the importance of looking within myself for answers it wasn't until the Tesco incident and the media furore it ignited that I realized all this time I had been looking for answers in all the wrong places. Founding Jediism had not given me the inner peace I thought it would. I was still a work in progress and inner peace was my future not my present.

SWEPT AWAY

Although I realized soon after the Tesco incident that I had let myself and Jediism down, the media interest simply intensified. With constant demands on my time, and my ego drawn to the spotlight like a moth to a flame, I didn't give myself a chance to reflect and regroup. Everybody wanted to get in touch with me. I was so conditioned to saying yes to every request, because I thought that was how to get Jediism on the map, that I kept on saying yes.

Jediism was national news again but this time it triggered a major backlash within the church. My followers started to question why I was courting negative publicity in this way. I was invited onto countless forums to explain myself and did a number of high-profile radio and TV interviews and phone-ins. and appeared on shows like Nicky Campbell's *Big Question*. During these, other religious sects were vocal in their opposition. I found myself rising to the opposition but this wasn't who I was. This wasn't Jediism. I did not feel comfortable with the way this was all heading. It started to eat me up. I felt defeated. Jediism was becoming an out of control monster and the catalyst a moment of stupid, impulsive behaviour in Tesco.

To make matters worse, if that were possible, within the Jediist movement itself I began to find myself the target of hate mail or accusations that were simply not true. It soon became clear that the media and everyone wanted to make far more of this than it was. It was time for me to make a decision, especially as I was still struggling to manage my as yet undiagnosed Asperger's and dyslexia limited my ability to communicate effective responses in writing. I was having meltdowns on a regular basis and my family were concerned I might do myself serious harm. I could carry on being a reed blown in the weed and keep Jediism in the headlines or I could take a step back and reassess. The Jediist in me chose the latter option.

BACK TO BASICS

If founding the Church of Jediism in 2007 was my "New Hope" where there was the happy excitement of new beginnings, the Tesco incident in 2009 was my "Empire Strikes Back" moment when all around me seemed dark. The incident and my inappropriate ego-driven response made it clear that I needed to get back to basics. I had to work on my personal development and feel the Force within me, just as Luke travels to Dagobah to meet Yoda to learn how to control the Force.

There is a pivotal scene in *The Empire Strikes Back* when Luke goes into a cave and has a vision where he encounters Darth Vader and discovers his own face beneath Vader's mask. Luke sees clearly at this moment that he is the problem and that the way forward is to work on himself. After losing my temper and then going national for the most trivial of reasons, I knew by the end of 2009 that it was time for the leader of the Church of Jediism, a new movement that hoped to embody the positive change it wanted to inspire in others, to have a good long hard look at himself.

I knew the theory and could talk a good game but when given an opportunity to live what I preached and resolve a conflict with harmony, I had lost my temper and let my ego take over. I did not behave like a Jediist Master. So in early 2010 I made the decision to turn away from the glare of the media spotlight and focus on my own personal development. I trusted that I would just know when the time was right to return to my role as active church leader. Right now I accepted that I was too young. If Jediism was to make a positive mark on the world and be taken seriously, it was vital that I was mature and in control.

To say this period in my life was my dark night of the soul isn't an exaggeration as there were moments when I thought about shutting down the church completely. It had become an albatross around my neck. I was recognized everywhere I went as "the *Star Wars* boy" or the arrogant guy who wanted to start a new world religion. It was all way too much for me to process. Some days I couldn't even face going outside because of the attention I knew I would get. I had thousands of followers online but I was very much alone. I vented my frustration by bashing out letters on the computer, or kicking and thumping tables so violently I broke my toes and my fingers. I'd find myself in the emergency room at the local hospital yet again with another unexplained injury. I told them I was a skateboarder.

Whereas previously I had accepted every media opportunity to promote the church, from 2010 onwards I started to withdraw. My meltdowns were increasing in intensity and I needed to sort them out before my family took drastic action. In the early days of the church requests for interviews and appearances were wildly exciting but having done so many now there was no excitement for me anymore. I had lost faith in myself and didn't actually know what I was trying to achieve with the church. I had founded it when I was 21 but three years later I wasn't the same person anymore.

I began to turn down requests for interviews or appearances on major shows which I would have jumped at the chance of doing before because they would have brought massive publicity to the church. *Big Brother* contacted me but I didn't have any desire within me to do it. I felt weak and in need of time to gather strength.

Of course, I couldn't stop doing interviews and requests for information about the church altogether. If I had done that, it would have suggested that I was abandoning Jediism and letting down all those who had signed up and put their faith in me. I hadn't abandoned Jediism. Far from it. I wanted to immerse myself in it more actively than ever before. I just needed time and space to find out what was going on inside me, and to use that period of reflection to create inspiring church scripture that was based on real-life experience not theory. So I set up an online automatic system on the church website to send downloads of information and advice to my existing followers but didn't actively try to recruit new members. I devoted my time and energy not to media appearances but to developing greater inner strength and true understanding of what it means to be a Jediist. It was what I needed to do at the time. The right thing for me was to withdraw and focus on understanding myself better.

Immersing myself in performing arts studies at college gave me the confidence to trust that one day, if I got enough study credits, I might be able to study for a degree in a subject I had a natural affinity for because it is all about endless discovery: science. That long-term goal became a reality when I was 25. Not long after the Tesco incident, I scored a surprisingly high mark in a maths test and was offered the opportunity to read a chemistry degree. That was a beautiful moment in my life, but unfortunately my intensely odd behaviour still kept raising its head and causing problems. It unsettled and alienated everybody around me. My moods would suddenly dip. I would have intense panic attacks. I would cry, punch and pull my hair out for no reason. My behaviour alarmed my family but they simply didn't know what to do.

Mercifully, I have never been a danger to anyone but myself so although my behaviour was a cause for concern I was still able to function. Deep down though, I longed for understanding of what exactly was going on with me. I did voluntarily seek out counselling for my feelings of being overwhelmed or not being able to cope with stress and episodes of agoraphobia (fear of public spaces). I ended up having this bizarre love/hate relationship with counselling: I loved that it calmed me down temporarily but hated that it didn't resolve anything in the long term. I still didn't know why I was having anxiety and meltdowns. Each time I met a new counsellor they wanted to hear everything about me. They would listen and listen as I talked and talked. I would sense light at the end of the tunnel but then the panics and the anxieties would return. Nobody could work it out!

When I started this inward journey of self-understanding and growth at the age of 23 I had no idea how long it would take. Seven years later I realize that it is a journey that will never end – as the life of a Jediist is one of endless self-discovery – but in my seven years of exile I had some powerful breakthroughs in self-awareness. In the pages that follow I will offer these insights to you in the humble hope they will guide and empower your spiritual growth in the same practical way they did mine.

Recognizing that I was vulnerable and had trigger points, the first step for me was to learn how to remain calm and in control in tense situations. Jediism gave me a theoretical framework or philosophical understanding to approach life but I urgently needed practical and everyday guidelines about self-defence. The obvious place to look was in the world of martial arts training.

The life of a Jediist is one of endless self-discovery.

Life blessed me with a father who was a martial arts master, and so when I was growing up, martial arts training was something I had little choice but to learn about. I remember watching my father practising his exercises at home and teaching crowded classes of eager students. I got a personal introduction to martial arts through him but as it was my father's area of expertise and I wanted to make my own mark in the world I didn't throw myself into it fully. Humbled and eager to learn now because of the bruising experience I had been through with Tesco, I took a leap of faith and asked my father for advice to deepen and mature my understanding.

Rather than sit me down and talk – big emotional conversations are just not his way – my father simply recommended some books about martial arts and encouraged me to work through them at my own pace. He suggested I listen to them via an audio recording and concentrate on every word. At this point I was willing to give anything a try. It was the best decision an angry young man could make because martial arts are not about fighting at all but about peace.

LIFE-GIVING SWORD

Martial arts or the way of the warrior has its roots in ancient cultures. The Romans, Chinese, Japanese, Greeks, Celts, Norse and many others all revered their warriors not just for their skill in combat but because of their prowess in all aspects of human life – physical, mental and spiritual.

For those who follow the way of the warrior, training is not just about combat and technical skill but about the spirit in which they live their life. For example, the Japanese Samurai warriors are required to meditate on their own death every

> # *Weapons do not win battles. Your mind powerful it is.*
>
> Yoda, *Star Wars: The Clone Wars*

day to help them stay grounded in their human existence. They must also dedicate themselves to appreciating art and culture as a reminder of the beauty of life they are defending. In addition, the physical discipline of daily combat training and practice is required so that they are always prepared to protect the vulnerable and defenceless. However, a true warrior will practise the art of peace not war and always act in ways that honour the soul, avoiding combat if possible. The greatest warrior is the one who does not ever enter into combat because a mark of their skill is not winning battles but finding ways to defuse or avoid difficult situations.

The way of the warrior must be one of peace, and my studies of martial arts taught me something I thought I knew but truly didn't: a Jediist does not need to retaliate or go into physical or emotional combat when challenged. They can win by their calm presence alone. Anytime there is aggression, a trigger is pulled or a fist is thrown in retaliation, the dark side of the Force is energized and that is the mistake I made in Tesco. I felt I was being unjustly treated and I responded with aggression.

If I was able to perceive situations I encountered in this peaceful and calm way then combat and tension need not ever occur, as I could handle difficult situations through spirit and intuition instead of anger. This martial arts spirit could permeate all areas of my life and allow for mindful and peaceful reactions to every stimulus, be it someone squaring up for a fight or the frustration of delayed trains or the demands of others. In martial arts this is known as the "life-giving sword".

This was another road to Damascus moment for me. Jediism was a perfect opportunity for the modern truth seeker to be reintroduced to the ancient spiritual way of the warrior. I didn't see it fully before but I did now. Becoming a Jediist is announcing to the world that you are an aware and peaceful human being who respects all life and sees that we are all one in spirit. A Jediist is someone who unifies body, mind and spirit, and understands the power of his or her thoughts, feelings, words and actions to make the world a better place. If a Jediist can maintain the same watchful presence of mind that a martial artist has in their training this will result in a meaningful and sincere life.

All along, the missing piece of the puzzle was right under my nose but I just hadn't been able to see it until the universe humbled me. My father's lifelong passion for martial arts was pointing me in the right direction from childhood but I hadn't noticed. It was only when my life was falling apart that I looked for inspiration to someone who was distant but always seemed so together – my father. Previously I had thought that martial arts and spirituality were opposites as one is seemingly violent and combative and the other is peace loving and gentle but I realized now that they were interlinked. It was time for me to pick up my sword, metaphorically speaking, and actually start to learn some physical martial arts techniques.

Sensing my sincere desire to learn, my father taught me physical sword techniques and how to focus strength and defuse dangerous situations. You avoid danger at all costs. What is self-defence? It is avoiding danger. The only time to fight is when there is absolutely no other option and it is fight or die. In all other situations the loving and compassionate response is to walk away. Attacking your enemy just energizes the dark side.

A Jediist does not need to retaliate or go into physical or emotional combat when challenged.

At this point in my life the church could have gone in any direction, perhaps even the dark side, but with my newfound understanding of martial arts I protected it and kept it safe. I could have vigorously defended Jediism and attacked my critics and probably gained followers for all the wrong reasons. Instead I decided to do nothing, let it go and trust the universe.

GENTLE HEALING

In order to heal the world's ills you must first heal your own wounds. There's absolutely no point trying to bring positive change into the world if you don't have self-knowledge or inner peace. Ultimately, combat-style martial arts weren't for me as I'm not a natural athlete like my father, but I learned so much from his tuition and we have both become closer as a result. Sensing that the way of the warrior was the way to begin my inner healing, I found a gentler form of martial arts that suited me and that was Tai Chi. There are many forms of martial arts that can lead to inner peace but when you are in a state of personal crisis and this is affecting you mentally, physically and emotionally, Tai Chi is the most calming holistic or all-round therapy. For the next five years it became my daily sanctuary and inspiration.

If you've never practised Tai Chi the only thing you probably know about it is from seeing people do weird slow-motion exercises in your local park. It may surprise you to learn that Tai Chi is indeed a martial art in that it is a movement meditation. Although martial arts are based on combat techniques they are first and foremost a means for body and mind to move in slow motion harmony, with tips and tricks to use to avert danger.

THE ART OF TAI CHI

Tai Chi is an ancient Chinese martial art practised for its health benefits, defence training and internal healing powers. It is recognized by its slow flowing movements with mental focus, breathing and relaxation and evolved in agreement with many Chinese philosophical principles including Taoism. Tai Chi movements if practised quickly can be a form of combat or self-defence. It has become international and has many modern styles but all trace their development back to Chen Village over 350 years ago. It is also believed that focusing the mind solely on the movements helps to bring about a state of mental calm and clarity. A number of research studies have confirmed that Tai Chi may be useful in improving health, balance and reducing stress.

Source: www.health.harvard.edu/staying-healthy/the-health-benefits-of-tai-chi

This is quite a difficult concept for people today to understand. We live in a competitive and fast-paced world, but if you live your life in this combative mode, not only do you feed the dark side with anger and tension and the desire to be the best, but you will also be defeated, as there will always be someone better or stronger than you. You will also constantly be engaged in confrontation because you are projecting confrontation to the universe and you attract into your life what you project.

Learning Tai Chi empowered me. It underlined the importance of discipline, correct breathing, slowing down, being aware of the present moment and, above all, connecting with the energy of Chi (the Force) from within because in life the greatest challenges are our own fear and tension. It taught me that the greatest battle is the one within myself and winning isn't the goal. The journey is the goal and the journey in martial arts is the one that goes within.

I learned discipline and focus from repeating those slow-motion body movements. I also learned to value every precious moment of my life as we never know which moment will be our last. Losing people I loved like my cousin Jo underlined that point and gave me a whole new appreciation of every breath I take.

Last, but by no means least, I also learned to develop a healthy sense of gratitude and to respect everything and everyone in my life. Gratitude and respect are key elements in martial arts training because they encourage us to be alert to the positive things going on around us and to interpret negative situations in a more positive and productive way. It's impossible to feel negative and grateful at the same time.

So from 2010 onwards I immersed myself in Tai Chi and along the way discovered in this movement meditation a peace of mind that had been lacking before. I learned that if you are not seeking conflict or tension you will not encounter it and if you do encounter it you will have the presence of mind to resolve it with harmony. People who try to intimidate or devalue or use you for their own selfish gain will have no power over you anymore.

There are going to be times when turning the other cheek isn't appropriate and you feel called as a Jediist to speak up, make your point or answer back or turn the spotlight on injustice or defend the weak from injustice. However, you should only do this if you are coming from a position of calm and understanding and never from a place of emotional turbulence as it will backfire and simply feed the dark side of the force. A Jediist fights the dark side not by engaging with it but by always shining light, peace and love into it.

LESSON SIX: MEANINGFUL LIVING

Read silently or, better still for the energizing and ritualizing impact, read out loud to yourself the following teaching and then incorporate the practical suggestions into your daily life. Making a commitment to those suggestions is essential otherwise this book is nothing but ideas and words. Too many people get stuck in the "thinking about it" stage but never find the courage or the discipline to do anything about their grand ideas. A Jediist has courage; a Jediist has self-discipline; and a Jediist will also live or embody what he or she believes. If you are to evolve into a Jediist you must move from theory to action as soon as possible. You must both be and do. There is no "I could" or "I might".

The Sixth Teaching on the Force

It is a blessing to have your absolute attention. May what you read or hear now help you to grow in discipline and self-awareness so you know what your true path in life is and where you can find the answers you are seeking.

What is your purpose? What is your meaning? What is life?

The way of the Jediist is one that offers you answers to these eternal questions, so that, rather than feeling like you are a ship tossed about on the ocean with no sense of direction, you are able to plot your course and destination. You will regain a sense of control and be able to navigate your way to enlightenment.

A Jediist knows that what they seek is within and that their own internal contradictions are their true enemy. To defeat your external enemies is good but the Jediist who defeats him or herself is the greatest of all warriors. One of the most powerful ways to confront yourself is to think about your own death. Treat every day of your life as the life or death situation it is because none of us knows for sure when we will die. This isn't to say you must live in a state of perpetual stress but rather in a state of alertness, gratitude and appreciation for the precious gift of life, the present moment that is unrepeatable and truly unique.

Living your life with an awareness of the inevitability of death takes the fear of death away. Freedom from the paralysing fear of death releases great power and connects you to the energy of the Force. If you focus on the fact that each act and word could be your last, you will find that your words and actions have great meaning and significance and your vital energy and courage will inspire all you encounter. It is often said that we are not truly prepared to live until we are prepared to die. Life assumes a greater meaning and purpose when we fully appreciate the fact we are going to die. Our death is real and will be marked by a specific day on the calendar. All the days leading up to that one assume a special significance. Time passes so quickly.

Knowing one day you will die – and that day could well be today – is not morbid but an empowering way to live. There will be no room for timidity or fear anymore because you will know that fear is only a thought in your mind. Being afraid prevents you from living in harmony with the Force within and all around you.

Living in harmony with the Force and freeing your mind from fear and limitation so that you can see you are connected to everything and everyone in the universe is the beating heart of Jediism. In this way every Jediist is liberated beyond life and death and connected to the Force in that they do not identify with their thoughts or emotions. They are able to step away from their egos and understand that if there is a yearning towards something or someone, they are not in control anymore, but rather what they are yearning for is in control of them. A Jediist is always in control because they know that inner peace is the only destination worth yearning and fighting for.

Every moment of your life you have an opportunity to discover inner peace and connect to the Force. Remember the powerful role of your thoughts and emotions in attracting what you want into your life, and so focus your intentions on love and compassion, and if negative thoughts and emotions strike, walk calmly through them. The way of the Jediist requires commitment, self-discipline, humility, focus, patience and being open to a feeling of connection with the universe and finding yourself in every moment. You must embrace, accept and rise above anger, fear, frustration and loss of focus, and accept these trials as a natural part of spiritual growth. In the process something truly miraculous will happen. You will feel calm and confident and in control. You will feel alive. You will become intimate with the present moment and in those intimate and loving moments you will become one with the force. You will be a Jediist.

Hold this prayer close to your spirit at all times.

A JEDIIST PRAYER FOR THE JOURNEY OF A JEDIIST

May you remember that the power exerted by the fist is temporary, but the strength of the mind and spirit last forever. This is the journey of the Jediist.

May you have the courage to remember all your Jedi training and use your training to defend and help the weak and defenceless with a heart that is wise and forgiving. This is the journey of the Jediist.

When you are challenged, may you focus on love and peace and always seek harmony and light. This is the journey of the Jediist.

May you find the strength of mind and body always to do what is required with honour, and to walk away rather than retaliate in a situation that cannot be resolved peacefully. This is the journey of the Jediist.

May you remain humble and know that mistakes can be priceless opportunities to find your path and connection to the force. This is the journey of the Jediist.

May you remain fully present, aware and alive in every moment. This is the journey of the Jediist.

May you rise above the fear of death and remember that you are in control of what you think and feel. This is the journey of the Jediist.

May you understand that your meaning is your journey and that your journey is your meaning.

Take a moment of reflection now to rejoice in your journey and be thankful for your life as a Jediist. As you do, feel the Force flow clearly through you.

To defeat your external enemies is good but the Jediist who defeats himself is the greatest of all warriors.

WAY OF THE JEDIIST GUIDELINES

1. Read ancient texts

We've seen that what sets a Jediist apart is their intelligence, they are curious and study more than most. So I'm going to recommend some more enlightening books. They are ancient texts and will require concentration because the language is not modern but they are worth the effort:

Plato's *Republic*: A Jediist takes an interest in politics and government and this book is absorbing.

Confessions by St Augustine: This is a book about living a humble, simple and pure life. It is the life story of a man who put morality before personal pleasure.

Tao Te Ching by Lao Tzu: Another ancient text a Jediist should seek out as it is discusses what true strength of character is.

The Book of Proverbs by King Solomon: An insightful and poetic text about living a wise and pure life, to be found in the biblical Old Testament.

Sun Tzu's *The Art of War*: A book about clever thinking and survival tactics.

2. Learn a martial art

Jediists are peaceful people but they are also called always to defend the vulnerable and helpless if a situation demands. If you are serious in your intention to become a Master Jediist you will need to learn or study a martial art not just for self-defence but also to underline the importance of discipline, patience and respect. You can watch some instructional videos on the Church of Jediism faculty but if you prefer to train in a more traditional way I recommend Kendo, Tai Chi, Kung Fu or Tae Kwon Do. It's important that you find a form of martial art that suits you.

Do some research online, watch *The Last Samurai* movie to inspire you and attend a few classes and if you prefer not to attend classes you can follow the training offered via the Church of Jediism or take your pick from the many wonderful online courses and instruction available. During your training, remember to use your skill in martial arts only to defend yourself and others.

If you prefer a martial art that is less athletic in its expression I highly recommend Tai Chi. A great place to start is with this book – one that inspired me: *Tai Chi: A Practical Approach to the Ancient Chinese Movement for Health and Well-Being* by Angus Clark.

Never forget that the true value of martial arts is not learning the physical exercises but the spiritual principles. Each exercise will teach you about the flow of universal life energy or the Force, and about intuition. Actions of blocking, deflecting and striking all contain concepts that apply to the human spirit. In combat you unite all these concepts because when under attack you are tested and your true self emerges. That is where you can truly learn about yourself.

3. Connect to the flow

Martial arts aren't the only physical discipline that incorporate a spiritual element. It is possible to learn the same lessons of discipline, awareness and creativity from sport, dancing, skating, running and other physical activities where you can connect to the flow of the universal life energy or force. If you can't engage in physical activity due to a medical condition, learning about martial arts and the spiritual component is completely valid. You may also find that non-physical creative pursuits like writing, painting, art, or learning a musical instrument or language are suitable alternatives because they also require the same patience, dedication, discipline and effort as martial arts. Committing to any hobby or activity teaches you so much more than just that hobby or activity. It teaches you a crucial life lesson: you only get out of something what you put into it, or life rewards those who do rather than think.

4. Journey into yoga

Try some yoga. Again you can sign up to a class or you can learn online or from a book. Like martial arts, yoga has manifold benefits – physical, mental, emotional and above all, spiritual. If you are looking for a starting point, try this book as it is one that captured my imagination: *Yoga Gym* by Nicola Jane Hobbs.

5. Life review

Take a few moments to sit quietly and think about what you

have achieved so far in your life. Think about both the good and the bad, the happiness and the regrets. Celebrate what you are proud of and forgive yourself for what you are not so proud of. Acknowledge that you made mistakes and there were things you could have done better, then forgive yourself. Make peace with your past. Forgive yourself for not knowing what you only know now. The definition of failure is to keep repeating the same mistakes, so tell yourself that from this day on you will use your increasing self-awareness and your knowledge of Jediism to make changes.

Don't set yourself up for failure by thinking you will never make mistakes again as without question, you are going to make mistakes. Indeed making mistakes is the only way you can continue to learn and grow. A Jediist is not perfect but imperfectly perfect. He or she is constantly evolving and growing and learning.

6. Meditate on death

The purpose of this meditation – which I recommend doing monthly – is to become aware of the fact that one day you are going to die. Your loved ones will die too because death is unavoidable. Meditating on this inevitability isn't morbid. It will help you make the most of every moment.

This meditation is about death but it is also about helping you prepare to live.

Find a place where you can get some peace and quiet. Listen to your breathing and relax. Allow thoughts to drift in and out of your mind. Then when you feel relaxed enough, think about your own death. What does dying mean to you? Are you afraid? When do you think you will die? What are the things you want to do before you die? What would your obituary say? How do you want everyone to remember you? What will people say about you at your funeral? What would you like them to say?

You may then want to move your thoughts to people you have known who have died. How did their death change you? If you haven't yet experienced the death of someone important to you, imagine what that would feel like for you and if you knew they were to die tomorrow what you would say to them now.

You may find yourself getting emotional during this mediation. Notice your feelings and let them flow through you. When you are prepared to live your life with the knowledge that you and those you love will one day die you stop taking your life and the lives of others for granted. You become authentic and sincere. Repeat this meditation the following month and see if your responses have changed.

I AM A JEDIIST

My father, Christopher Lawrence Jones, has five black belts in Karate and invented his own style of martial arts training inspired by Karate 30 years ago called Yamashima. He also holds a bachelor's degree in history and archaeology, is a qualified reflexologist and EFT practitioner, experienced mediator in domestic problem mediation and a Jediist Master.

Below, my father talks about his life in martial arts and how the Force inspired him to new levels of creativity.

The majority of my career was devoted to archaeological research and digs but I also specialized in EFT (emotional freedom technique) and have studied the practice to offer coaching sessions to help anyone I can. However, my passion in life has always been self-defence and martial arts. It was here that I felt the Force or universal life energy flow most strongly through me. It flowed so strongly that I decided I wanted to create my own martial arts system, called Yamashima.

Yamashima comes from my development of traditional Karate mixed with boxing techniques to create a practical self-defence system. I have taught this system with great success to packed halls of students in the UK for close to 30 years. Yamashima is an easy-to-learn Karate-based system that can help anyone, whatever their age or fitness level or experience of martial arts, become wise and practical in potentially dangerous situations. I decided to create the system because I wanted to offer something that I felt would speak to people who wanted to learn the ancient art of self-defence combined with modern self-defence techniques.

Learning Yamashima doesn't just teach a person how to defend themselves, it offers some life lessons, such as the importance of correct breathing, slowing down, being aware of the present moment and, above all, that conflict begins and ends from within. Even in great fights the greatest challenge is our own fear and tension.

The sparrow never lands where the tiger roams. A Jediist knows that conflict cannot continue without her or his participation.

Daniel M. Jones

Chapter
SEVEN

Counselling, Stress Management and Control

Named must your fear be before banish it you can.

Yoda, from the novelization of *Star Wars Episode III: Revenge of the Sith*

The Force is strong with a Jediist who has an open heart and mind that sees loving connections between everyone and everything. But a Jediist must always be vigilant and aware that the dark side can be quicker, easier and more seductive than the light side. So, to protect themselves from the forces of darkness, Jediists must learn the art of self-defence.

As we saw in the last chapter, martial arts training is a perfect starting place for self-defence on both a physical and a spiritual level, but the ability to truly understand yourself is equally important when it comes to self-defence. If you aren't self-aware and don't know what your stress triggers are, you are going to be vulnerable to the dark side. Self-knowledge is the beginning of wisdom.

Despite having hit the headlines as the founder of the Church of Jediism I wasn't wise enough yet. I didn't know myself. I wasn't in control and inner calm is the hallmark of a Jediist. In short, I was vulnerable. There was still much for me to learn.

Inner calm is the hallmark of a Jediist.

THE BEGINNING OF WISDOM

As soon as I started to practise Tai Chi on a regular basis I did notice an inner peace that had been lacking before but there was still a way to go. My thoughts still flew around my head with rapid and uncontrollable speed. I still got irrationally upset and angry and spoke before thinking. I still had meltdowns. I didn't understand myself and didn't feel in control of my words and actions and that unpredictability made me fearful of myself.

My mood would often dip inexplicably or I would get wound up about the most trivial of things; for example, if there were delays or changes to my daily routines. I simply couldn't understand why the small stuff threw me off course so dramatically. But then the universe sent me the explanation I had been waiting my whole life for. On 23 June 2013, at the age of 26, I was officially diagnosed with Asperger's syndrome.

TEXT BOOK

All these years when I sought counselling the fact that I might be on the autism spectrum never occurred to me until early 2013 when a friend of a friend, who was an autism specialist, said that it might be something for me to look into. He encouraged me to do an autism questionnaire online. When my score of over 38 placed me firmly in the autism spectrum I immediately made an appointment to see my doctor. The diagnosis was confirmed and I got the answer, the explanation, I had been seeking my entire life. I had Asperger's syndrome.

I was assessed at various mental health clinics and by an autism specialist and a psychologist who all confirmed the diagnosis again and again. The relief was overwhelming. This was it. This was the explanation. My fear had been named at last. I wasn't mad, bad or disturbed. I had a medical condition and the way forward was to understand it fully and find ways to manage it.

I can't express fully in words what a relief being diagnosed with Asperger's was. Until my diagnosis I knew very little about the condition and, like most people, thought it was some kind of disability or mental illness. It most certainly is not. It is a neurodevelopmental disorder on the autism spectrum.

I soon found out that autism spectrum disorder (ASD) is a group of disorders characterized by poor motor skills, lack of empathy, obsession with narrow interests and a fixation on routine. Panic attacks are likely if that routine is disrupted. Asperger's syndrome is on the higher functioning end of the autism spectrum. In other words, although I can function in society, most people would regard me as odd because my condition increases the likelihood of me behaving in an inappropriate way. People with Asperger's tend to talk and think too fast and take things too literally. We can't understand sarcasm and the importance of eye contact in a conversation, and we often feel out of place or uncomfortable in social situations or gatherings.

Text-book description of me!

CALM AND IN CONTROL

There is currently no cure for Asperger's but many approaches, therapies and interventions that can improve quality of life. These may include stress management, behavioural therapy, counselling and dietary changes.

One of the huge frustrations of Asperger's is obsessive behaviour which can manifest in weird routines such as turning a cup three times before drinking or not walking on pavement lines. I can relate! Something in my head tells me that disaster will strike if I don't do these kinds of weird routines. An outsider looking in might think that it would be easy for me simply to snap out of it but it's impossible. Let me compare it to someone telling you that you must never sneeze again. You can't promise them that because you can't control sneezing any more than an Asperger's sufferer can control their obsession with routine. It is a frustrating neurological disorder.

To this day I can't eliminate my obsessive and unusual behaviour but I have learned ways to control it and it is all down to how your mind perceives things. Change your thoughts and you change your life, and this crosses over to Jediism, of course. My Asperger's diagnosis forced me to examine carefully my thought patterns and their impact on my actions and my life. It became absolutely clear to me that thought management was the secret of a fulfilled life. We experience the world we create with our thoughts.

While learning about Asperger's and ways to manage it I realized that a lot of the thought and behaviour management advice could be extraordinarily helpful for anyone, whether they had Asperger's or not. I decided it was essential to include thought management in the Church of Jediism scripture applied living techniques. A Jediist needs to learn how to be always calm and in control of their thoughts, feelings and actions. In the words of Yoda in *The Empire Strikes Back*: "Control, control, you must learn control."

A BLESSING AND A CURSE

Just as there is night and day and a dark and light side of the Force, my condition is both a curse and a blessing. A curse in that it caused me and people who cared about me a lot of anxiety and confusion, but a blessing in that I have the ability to make connections others might miss.

Another symptom of Asperger's is the ability to recognize patterns: my brain is constantly trying to make sense of the environment and a break in that pattern is glaringly obvious to me. This explained why I found it hard to settle into school and struggled with grades but excelled when there was anything to do with pattern problems, such as art or music or science. It also explained why I was never happier than when analysing numbers or data and why I lost control or had meltdowns whenever my daily routine was disturbed. I wasn't weird. I had Asperger's and my resulting ability to see patterns or the bigger picture inspired me to create Jediism.

Detecting similarities in all the religious and philosophical systems in the world, my pattern-seeking brain instantly connected those similarities to the concept of the Force in *Star*

Wars. My knowledge of the *Star Wars* universe was extreme.
I sensed an opportunity to bring spirituality to a potentially
massive audience in an exciting, modern and fun way. In short,
Asperger's is the reason the Church of Jediism was born in
the mind of a boy from Wales who wanted to find a system to
understand not just himself but life, the universe and everything.

MY CALLING

With hindsight I can see that my Asperger's diagnosis truly set
me free. Not only did it give me the self-understanding I had
previously lacked, it also gave me a sense of purpose and
direction I hadn't had before. Knowing who I was and why I
behaved the way I did meant I didn't want to hide anymore. I
wasn't perfect but I didn't need to be. Just because I founded
a church didn't mean that I had to be a perfect human
being. Spiritual guides or teachers are just like everyone else
– the only difference being that they feel it is their calling to
encourage others to search for meaning in their lives – and
to see them in any other way is damaging to your spirituality.
I am not some superior being. I have flaws. I am a work in
progress as we all are.

I appreciate that my approach here is unusual as in certain
circles the ancient idea that a guru is someone without flaws, or
someone who had flaws once but has left them firmly behind,
still persists. Who wants to listen to or follow a guide who hasn't
conquered their own demons? I challenge this old-fashioned
tradition and feel it is my calling to be as emotionally honest

as possible and to let my followers know that I'm certainly not perfect. I'm learning and growing with them.

We all have flaws and weaknesses and need to learn to accept ourselves, warts and all. Sometimes we say or do things we regret. Sometimes we get things wrong. Sometimes we are weak and needy. Sometimes we disappoint those we love, and in a world with billions of people there is always going to be someone cleverer, thinner, better-looking, younger or more successful. That's life. So if you have convinced yourself that you just aren't good enough, you need to stop right there. Perfection in this life is not possible – indeed it is not even desirable because if you were perfect there would be no opportunity for growth. Remember, being a Jediist is all about evolution. I've managed to turn what many might perceive as a weakness – my Asperger's – into a strength, and I truly believe each one of us can transform our weaknesses into strengths and setbacks into opportunities. We learn and grow not from our successes and perfections but from our failures and our flaws.

I'm most certainly not perfect but I don't need to be and neither does anyone who joins my church. The spiritual life isn't about getting it right all the time. It is about getting it wrong some of the time and learning and growing from your mistakes. It is about confronting your demons and accepting that there is always room for improvement because nobody can or should be perfect.

Just imagine how dull and limiting the world would be if everyone was perfect! How could you grow spiritually if you didn't have inner conflicts to resolve? Joining the Church of

ASPIE WORLD

As soon as I was diagnosed with Asperger's I immediately made a point of finding out everything I could about the condition. I listened to audiobooks, attended talks and lectures, and met and bonded with some amazing people also suffering from my condition. I was incredibly disappointed, though, by the information that was available online. There was just nothing there. Just as religion had not given me the answers or fulfilment I sought, leading me to found Jediism online, I decided to create my own YouTube channel with information and advice for Asperger's sufferers. In 2014 I filmed my first YouTube video just talking about my experiences and created a YouTube channel called Aspie World.

If you are interested in finding out more about Aspie World, where I show the world life as an Aspie through a series of videos and discuss matters and interests for anyone with autism spectrum disorder, do visit www.theaspieworld. com. From there you can find links to my YouTube channel as well as Facebook, Instagram and Twitter and my vlog.

Jediism is joining a community of people who are committed to growth and constantly evolving into higher and higher manifestations of themselves. The sky – the galaxy – is the limit.

From my diagnosis in 2013 onwards I threw my energy into understanding my Asperger's, myself and enriching my life. I composed and performed music with my band Straight Jacket Legends and in 2016 was signed by not one but two record labels, with my debut album *Go Bananas* charting in Japan. Alongside all this I completed my chemistry degree. Throughout these years Jediism was still calling my name but I hadn't yet sensed that the time was right to reactivate the church fully. I trusted that I would know when that time came but perhaps the reason I wasn't yet ready to go ahead was that there was one final piece of the puzzle missing for me. That missing piece of the puzzle is the subject of the next chapter.

LESSON SEVEN: CONTROLLED LIVING

Read silently or, better still for the energizing and ritualizing impact, read out loud to yourself the following teaching and then incorporate the practical suggestions into your daily life. Making a commitment to those suggestions is essential otherwise this book is nothing but ideas and words. Too many people get stuck in the "thinking about it" stage but never find the courage or the discipline to do anything about their grand ideas. A Jediist has courage; a Jediist has self-discipline; and a Jediist will also live or embody what he or she believes. If you are to evolve into a Jediist you must move from theory to action as soon as possible. You must both be and do. There is no "I could" or "I might".

The Seventh Teaching on the Force

It is a blessing to have your attention because what you will read or hear now is about facing your greatest fear. Every Jediist must name this fear because if they cannot they will not become one with the Force.

What is this fear, you may ask? Is it death? Is it poor health? Is it loneliness? Is it failure? It is none of these things. Your greatest fear is not that you will one day die or that you will go through periods of poor health and loneliness or experience failure in your life. All these challenges are natural and inevitable parts of our human journey, and from them we learn and grow and our connection to the Force strengthens. Our greatest and deepest fear is that there is infinite potential within and all around us. It is not our disappointments, pain and suffering that we fear but our potential to be infinitely brilliant, creative and beautiful.

Each one of us is a child of the universe no less than the trees and the stars, and each one of us has the right to a wonderful life. To draw inspiration from Marianne Williamson's book, *Return to Love*, hiding our light does not make the light of others shine brighter. There is nothing noble about diminishing yourself so that other people won't feel threatened by you. We were born to reveal the light that shines within us. That inner light is not just in some of us, but in everyone, and as each Jediist glows from within they inspire others to do the same, lighting up the world one Jediist at a time. Naming our fear and becoming a shining light liberates others to do the same.

Nothing diminishes our light more than stress and pressure. Many of us lead increasingly busy lives and not having the tools and techniques to deal with that pressure can cause chaos and meltdown. Jediism provides those tools and techniques. There is no better way to rise above the pressures in your life than to move in harmony with the Force. A Jediist Master is not immune to pressure – as life is pressure – but he or she faces it with courage knowing that peace of mind can be found during times of tension.

Tension is inevitable and the first way to balance stress is to understand who you are. If you don't understand yourself you won't be coming from a position of strength and others will manipulate you into being what they want you to be. A Jediist knows who they are and that their purpose in life is to find inner calm through their connection to the Force and to use that connection to help and inspire others.

The dark side loves to see a Jediist collapse under pressure because if it can disturb your balance, it can sneak into your heart and your mind to produce fear and insecurities, and destroy your inner light or calm. The good news is you do not have to let the dark side in. You do not need to succumb to fear or poor health under pressure. You simply need to find time to be still and at one with yourself and the Force. In those quiet moments you will discover your infinite potential.

Every Jediist should make moments during their day to be still and remind themselves that they are not what is outside themselves but what is within. They are spiritual beings having a human experience. This inward looking starts first thing in the morning, when there are instant demands on your time. A Jediist will always take a quiet moment of reflection before rushing to meet these demands because they know that maintaining peace of mind is absolutely vital. They know that they don't have to be torn into pieces by stress and pressure and that they can find peace of mind in any situation because stress and pressure are illusions to a Jediist.

The only reality to a Jediist is spirit – their loving connection to the Force. They allow themselves moments of reflection during the day to nurture this connection to the Force and see the bigger picture of love interconnecting everyone and everything. They set aside time for themselves in solitude and during these moments of peace and reflection they exchange heaviness for joy. It is like coming up for air after a period of submersion when all pressure is released but these moments of joy and peace cannot happen until they pause, turn down the volume of their lives and are still and at harmony with themselves in the moment.

A Jediist makes self-knowledge a priority.

You see, my friends, the great majority of stresses in our lives are caused by our inability simply to be comfortable with ourselves. One of the reasons we are uncomfortable is that we don't understand ourselves, haven't taken the time to figure ourselves out and seek our identity from others or external sources.

A Jediist makes self-knowledge a priority because he or she knows self-knowledge is truly the beginning of wisdom. I encourage you all to make it a personal practice to spend a few minutes completely alone to reflect each day. A Jediist enjoys his or her own company as much as he or she enjoys the company of others. You may not think it is possible to find that alone time in the midst of all the hustle and bustle of life but you can. You may not think it is possible to find inner calm but it is. This inner calm will empower you to find peace under pressure and by so doing to become the Force.

Take a few moments now to be still and absorb the words of this prayer for inner peace.

A JEDIIST PRAYER FOR INNER PEACE

May peace of mind and calm always be mine whatever situation, tension or pressure I find myself in. When my mind and heart are troubled my life is like a turbulent ocean, and my lack of direction and balance lead me to the dark side of the Force. But when there is stillness, strength and clarity of mind I can turn away from the darkness and find the light.

May I be guided towards the light always and may I trust that this light will heal my stress and deliver me from tension, just as I trust the sun to rise each day after the darkness of the night.

May I understand that when I find inner peace and trust myself to seek the light during times of stress and chaos I am truly one with the Force. I am a Jediist and I am powerful beyond measure.

A Jediist knows that their purpose in life is to find inner calm through their connection to the Force and to use that connection to help and inspire others.

CONTROLLED LIVING GUIDELINES

1. Read calming books

The Little Book of Mindfulness by Dr Patrizia Collard is about the concept of mindfulness – finding inner calm by living in the present moment – and has clear guidance on how to use this skill. Really easy to read and a wonderful resource to help every Jediist cope with anxiety, stress and tension.

Another book I found helpful is *Change Your Thinking with CBT* by Dr Sarah Edelman. It's all about noticing how your thoughts are actually creating stress and tension in your life and changing your thoughts to find inner peace. It is based on the principles of cognitive behaviour therapy (CBT), a psychological tool used by therapists to aid people develop realistic thought patterns that will help them respond better to upsetting emotions. This book will show you how to challenge voices of fear and doubt in your head, and deal calmly and rationally with feelings of anger, depression, frustration and anxiety.

2. Take five

It's often the simplest of things that can be the most effective, and one technique I recommend when you are feeling stressed and tense is a breathing exercise. We all tend to breathe shallowly when we are anxious and this limits blood flow and oxygen supply to your brain so you can't think clearly. The next time you are stressed take a huge, deep breath in through your nose and fill your lungs to capacity. Then breathe out through your mouth. Repeat this five times and I guarantee you will feel calmer and more in control.

3. Relieve the pressure

This next simple exercise can help ease stress when you feel overwhelmed.

Lightly place the palm of one hand on your forehead directly above your eyes or about an inch or so above your eyebrows. Take a deep breath and allow all the stressful feelings and thoughts to flow through you. Don't try to fight them with positivity; just drop into your stress. Keep breathing deeply and stay focused for two to three minutes. You may notice as you do that you feel strong pulses in the palm of your hand resting on your forehead. This is positive as it means you are lifting out the stress and beginning to think more clearly and reconditioning your response to negative thoughts and feelings. This is also an effective exercise to do if you have difficult memories that you can't seem to shed.

4. Make fitness a priority

Again the answer to stress often lies in the simplest of things. In my life I have found time and time again that going for a walk, preferably with my dog (pets are another great reliever of stress), is one of the fastest ways to ease stress. There's a reason why movement is such an effective tension easer.

Physical exercise is one of the most effective ways of relieving stress because when we exert ourselves physically, the body releases chemicals. These endorphins are similar to opiates but the difference is these are natural substances produced by our own bodies and totally free of side effects, except for making us feel good. When it comes to stress management don't think you have to join a gym or commit to a tough exercise regime; simply try to do what you can, as every little bit helps.

Hopefully by now you will have incorporated martial arts into your life as that will certainly ease stress, but there are countless other ways to enjoy exercise and you need to find what suits you best. You may enjoy walking alone; you may enjoy exercising with others in a fitness class, cycling or running group. If you are competitive, you may enjoy sport such as football or tennis. All forms of exercise have physical benefits – and a healthy body equals a healthy mind – but for stress relief, exercising in natural surroundings has the most benefits because exposure to daylight has been proven successfully to boost mood.

I'm no fitness expert but I do know that to release endorphins and ease stress you need to get your heart beating faster than normal with aerobic exercise (running, fast walking, cycling etc.) for at least 15 minutes every day. If you can't manage 15 minutes there are still benefits to just a few minutes of brisk walking. Do check with your doctor, though, before undertaking any exercise programme, especially if you haven't exercised for a while, although walking is usually safe regardless of your fitness levels.

It's also a good idea to combine your aerobic exercise with some strengthening and stretching exercises. Strengthening exercises are muscle toning exercises, like push ups and sit ups, and they are important to prevent injury and keep your muscles and bones strong. Stretching exercises relax tense muscles and increase blood flow to the muscles. In my opinion, yoga is a great stretching exercise system for relieving stress. It also involves mind, body and spirit and includes breathing techniques that aid relaxation.

5. Spend time on yourself

Do something you find relaxing and which makes you feel good. This could be something as simple as taking a relaxing bath. having a massage, meeting friends or watching a funny movie. There is huge stress-relieving power in laughter so seek out the company of people who make you smile. It isn't selfish to devote some time out each day to yourself. Remember, you can't give to others what you don't have yourself, so find something that boosts your mood and then share your feelings of well-being with others.

6. Be one with the Force

Research has shown that meditation can reduce blood pressure and ease stress when you feel under pressure. It can alter the brain's neural pathways, making you more resilient to stress. Here's a simple one I recommend for all Jediists when they feel under stress as it has proved to be surprisingly effective for me and I hope it helps you too:

Close your eyes. Focus your attention on reciting out loud or silently, "I am one with the Force." Place one hand on your belly to sync the mantra with your breaths. Do this for around five minutes each day. Let any distracting thoughts float by like clouds.

7. Slow down

For five minutes focus all your attention on one activity completely. When you spend time in the present moment and don't let thoughts of the past or present distract you, you will immediately feel less tense. For example, if you are walking, notice the feel of the air on your face and how your arms swing by your side or the way your feet hit the pavement and so on. This is a mindfulness technique and you will learn more about mindfulness in the next chapter.

8. Reach out

Your friends and family and social media contacts are your network of support during times of stress. Reach out. Share. Don't suffer alone. If you don't feel you can talk to anyone talk to your doctor or phone a helpline. Remember, there are always opportunities to get a fresh perspective and words of support from your fellow Jediists within the Church of Jediism.

9. May the music be with you

Research shows that listening to soothing music can lower blood pressure, heart rate and anxiety. Music has a very powerful effect on your mood, so create a play list of songs that have a calming and uplifting effect. Listening to the sounds of nature – such as ocean waves or birds singing – and classical music can also be very soothing and you can find lots of those kinds of relaxation tracks on YouTube. You can also release tension by listening to fast, upbeat tunes or singing as loudly as you can in the shower, or whenever you want to let off steam. Remember, music is a powerful tool for a Jediist. It can raise your energy vibration and connect you to the power of the Force which is the essence of Jediism.

I AM A JEDIIST

Patrick "Custard Trout" Day Childs is living his dream, and probably the dream of anyone who loves gaming, as he reviews and writes about games for a living. He is a martial arts practitioner, Jediist-themed wedding coordinator, Jediist Master and Church of Jediism council member. Below he talks about how Jediism helped him deal with stress and depression in his life.

I first encountered the Church of Jediism when I was a teenager. It's a pretty standard story, I was stressed and depressed and they were there for me. But it went further than that. The founder Daniel Jones checked on me every single day, never asked for money or for me to become a Jediist. He never pressured me to join him. Instead, he pushed me to go out each day and helped me build a schedule to keep to.

Eventually I found myself in a much better place in life, and Jediism helped a lot with that journey. Through Jediism I learned to see each street for something beautiful. Really think about what those houses mean and represent. You might think of destroyed wildlife and mankind crushing things in its path. But Daniel taught me to see wonderful things, for each house there is a story, life, death, joy and sadness. He also encouraged me to see the beauty in nature and make sure I took time to go outside, connect with nature and open my mind and heart to new experiences. I visited aquariums, botanical gardens and grew plants. I woke up.

As I got to know Daniel I started to read his original Jediism training books. A lot of it made sense to me; Jediism can really genuinely help people.

As the years went on and I have lived by the Jediist code, it changed my life, day by day, bit by bit.

There is no emotion, there is peace – I began to approach each situation with a clear mind.

There is no ignorance, there is knowledge – I learn something new each day.

There is no passion, there is serenity – I cut down my hobbies and tried something new often.

There is no chaos, there is harmony – I keep a healthy schedule.

There is no death, there is the Force – each day I try to make a good lasting impact on people, so I can contribute to the Force and even in death people will feel my presence and care.

Jediism continues to change how I view the world every single day; I use the teachings from Jediism when bringing up my children. Every morning we read "What happened today" and learn about the history of each day. We also ensure we make at least two trips outside a week. We always explore our emotions and apply cognitive behavioural therapy, breaking our emotions into small easy-to-manage pieces that we can examine.

The Church of Jediism also encourages members to learn about other faiths, so I spent a lot of time visiting different places of worship, and it really opened my mind to the world, each offers really rich and interesting ideas. At this stage, I work with Daniel creating my own strands of Jediism. Daniel is deeply spiritual, but my strain of Jediism focuses on very practical techniques, and a much more atheist approach as there is a place within Jediism for all belief systems, including atheism.

The three major causes of stress are not knowing who you are, trying to change what can't be changed, and out of control thinking. A Jediist understands who they are, does not stress over what cannot be controlled or changed, and knows that their greatest weapon against stress is their ability to choose one thought over another.

Daniel M. Jones

Chapter
EIGHT

Healthy Living and Material Well-Being

Luminous beings are we, not this crude matter.

Yoda, *Star Wars Episode V: The Empire Strikes Back*

So far I've talked about connecting to the power of the Force with your mind and heart, but the missing part of the transformative spiritual equation here is your body. It took me until I was in my mid-twenties to appreciate just how important it is for my spiritual evolution to take care of my bodily health and all areas of my material well-being.

Inner calm can be achieved not just through martial arts training and stress management techniques discussed in previous chapters but also through physical well-being. In this chapter I'll explain how I truly learned to transform "this crude matter" into something "luminous" that could directly connect me to the Force.

You are probably expecting me to give some healthy diet guidelines now. I am sorry to disappoint: one thing I have learned along the way is that each one of us must find the kind of diet that is optimal for us. There is no one size that fits all.

GROWING UP AGAIN

As you've seen, 2010 to 2016 were the make-or-break years for Jediism. I knew I had to decide whether to drop it or make the movement grow up with me. I couldn't decide, so I made no decision and instead took a step back to work on my personal development, trusting increased self-awareness and control would guide me to the Force – as it did for Luke in the *Star Wars* saga.

During this time I was often plagued with great doubt. Crippled with indecision, I hid away. I like to give people my time, as that is the most precious gift you can give anyone, but during this tense period I would often lock myself away and requests for information would go unanswered.

At times my doubt grew so intense I was very close to dismantling the church as it felt like the sword of Damocles. To make matters worse there was opposition from rival Jedi groups and infighting within the church itself – it wasn't mature. The movement had to grow up if it was to evolve, just as I had to grow up. I did the odd radio and magazine interview here and there but generally tried to avoid publicity, even spectacular TV opportunities like appearing as a guest on *The Graham Norton Show* alongside *Star Wars'* Princess Leia, Carrie Fisher, in 2011. I regret not doing that now, especially since the tragic news of her death, but at the time it was the right decision. I didn't feel comfortable anymore in the public eye. I didn't feel good in my own skin and a lot of that was to do not just with my anxiety about the direction the church should head in, but with my general poor health and shambolic lifestyle. I was having panic meltdowns, putting on weight and suffering from hair loss.

YOU ARE WHAT YOU EAT AND DRINK

It's a common misconception that spirituality is separate or different from physicality, but that could not be further from the truth. I know that because one natural therapy for Asperger's that consistently achieves successful results is managing symptoms with nutritional supplements and dietary change. Without the gift of Asperger's I would never have had direct personal experience of just how powerful the connection between physical and emotional well-being is, and how what you put into your mouth impacts everything.

One of the most disruptive symptoms of Asperger's are panic and stress-related conditions such as insomnia, phobias and alopecia (hair loss). I suffered from all three! Sometimes my hair would fall out in clumps for days on end. Counselling gave me the cognitive tools to deal with anxiety and stress, and work on my sleep disruption and phobias, but it didn't help my hair grow back. Changing what I ate and taking supplements, including plant-based omega 3 oils, however, did have a dramatic impact for me.

When I was diagnosed with Asperger's I found out that diet can ease symptoms so I did some research and learned that I should take kelp, spirulina and zinc supplements for my hair loss, as well as increase my intake of fresh fruit and vegetables and cut down on processed foods and fast foods. Within a few weeks the effects were dramatic, and my hair was richer and stronger than before. Seeing how a few simple dietary changes changed the texture and thickness of my hair was the incentive for me to find dietary approaches to calm my mood in general. The resulting change in my overall well-being was astonishing and a wonderful side effect was that I lost weight too.

I wanted to find out more about diet and how it can impact physical, mental and emotional health, and so for the next two years I studied nutrition. It became clear to me that there were foods that could boost your mood, and foods that could drain it, and that it was entirely possible to boost your well-being with nutrition. It also became clear to me that the benefits of healthy eating extended to spiritual growth as unhealthy foods can lower your mood and by so doing block your connection to the Force. Seen in this light, every meal or snack you have has the potential to lift your mood and spirit, and connect you to the Force. Every meal is therefore potentially a sacred ritual.

We live in a fast food world. Many of us eat the wrong kinds of foods and too much of the wrong kinds of foods. Food is fuel. It can be the best kind of medicine but also the worst kind of poison, because every cell in your body is impacted by what you eat.

THE FLOW

A Jediist understands that physical health directly affects the flow of the Force within them and that poor health and depression suggest a block in the flow of the life Force. Eating right is therefore a powerful way to improve your spiritual health.

Your body is the sacred vessel which carries the internal universe of your thoughts and feelings. Your thoughts and feelings are incredibly important because they create your reality and your connection to the Force. If you don't take care of and respect your body, your connection to the Force will become limited because the mind and body have a powerful partnership. You can't divorce your physical health from your spiritual. If you are not eating well, it blocks the flow of universal life energy through your body.

When my diet was poor, my body wasn't getting the right nutrients and slipped into a slumber-like state that drained all energy from my mind and blocked my connection to the Force. I forgot that I was infinite creativity. I was on the way to becoming like the obese humans depicted in the Disney film *WALL-E* who simply don't move at all anymore, except to use their fingers to punch commands into a computer and eat processed food. However, when I found out that people with Asperger's should stay away in particular from alcohol as our tolerance for it is very low, and that a diet rich in processed foods, sweets, fizzy drinks, fries and so on is like waving a red rag to a bull, I changed my diet to a wholefood, organic diet. Within months I was losing weight and feeling lighter, both physically and spiritually.

I could feel the Force flowing strongly through me again.

NO ONE SIZE THAT FITS ALL

Of course, there are some obvious basics. We should eat more fresh food, fruit and vegetables, and less sugar and processed and fast foods. There are also certain superfoods that can aid brain power (see box) but every single human being is unique. I can't tolerate alcohol, coffee or chocolate and have to eat mostly organic foods to remain calm, but others can tolerate less healthy food choices.

The important thing is to do your research as I did and find what works for you. The indicator is always how fit, happy and healthy you feel. If you are a healthy weight and are bursting with energy and your skin feels clear, chances are your diet is a spiritual one. Your body and spirit are working in harmony with the Force.

JEDIIST SUPERNUTRIENTS

The following nutrients are required for the production of neurotransmitters and can boost concentration and brain power. They should be key players in the diet of every Jediist. You don't need to take supplements; just ensure your diet includes these food sources.

Vitamin B1 (thiamine) – whole grains, fruit, milk, cheese and eggs

Vitamin B5 (pantothenic acid) – pulses, broccoli, tomatoes and fruit

Vitamin B6 (pyridoxine) – chicken, fish, eggs, nuts, legumes

Vitamin B12 (cobalamin) – eggs, fish, dairy products

Folic acid – bananas, orange juice, strawberries, leafy vegetables, dried beans and peas

Iron – beef, whole grains, raisins, legumes and dried apricots

Calcium – leafy green vegetables, soya products, fish with bones, dairy products, nuts and seeds

Magnesium – whole grains, legumes, nuts and green vegetables

Potassium – apricots, avocados, bananas, grapefruit, prunes, strawberries, lean meat and fish

Zinc – beans, lentils, yeast, nuts, seeds, whole grain cereals

Omega 3 – oily fish, flax seeds, soya and walnuts

Source: www.ncbi.nlm.nih.gov/pmc/articles/PMC4772032/

BECOMING LUMINOUS

The old idea that your body is somehow separate from your spirit or lower or baser than spirit is wrong. Yoda describes the body as "crude matter" but that is only if we don't think of our bodies as vehicles for spirit. If we think of them as sacred vessels then our bodies become "luminous" or glowing with life Force energy. It is impossible to be healthy all the time, and some of us for reasons unknown are born with disabilities and health conditions that need to be managed all our lives, but in general the level of your health and well-being can say a great deal about your spiritual state.

A Jediist is healthy in mind, spirit and body. Of course, no one can be healthy 100 per cent of the time, but if you are frequently ill or depressed, it may suggest the need for some kind of change in your diet and lifestyle, and perhaps a change also in the way you think about yourself and your life. I don't think illness is all in the mind but I am inclined to believe that mindset can play a part in health and well-being. Studies have been done to suggest this may well be the case and in my own life I've seen how my mood impacts my physical well-being and the other way round. I do believe that thoughts create our world, but, having said that, I also know there are some things that can't be controlled by thought alone. For example, I was born with Asperger's and certainly didn't think that into existence, just as someone who is hit by a car doesn't attract that accident to themselves with their thoughts. It just happens.

In essence, while we cannot control absolutely everything that happens to us with our thoughts, we can control how we react to situations and how we take care of our physical health and material well-being. A Jediist focuses his or her attention not just on positive thinking and making positive diet and lifestyle choices but also on staying alert and prepared to deal with any situation that life throws at them. Paying attention to their material as well as their spiritual well-being is also an absolute priority.

MATERIAL WELL-BEING

The mark of a Jediist is not a dress code, tattoo or symbol, but health and joy in mind, body and spirit. If Jediists do encounter setbacks or poor health they face it with courage and see it as a tool for growth. Their good health manifests in all areas of their life. Balance and moderation are the key. They avoid drugs, alcohol and stimulants because when they are in harmony with the Force that is the only high they need. Sex is a natural high – a beautiful expression of love between two people and to be encouraged – but sex is something that should be earned not expected from others. A Jediist is typically faithful to one partner and not promiscuous.

A Jediist's living situation and finances will be healthy and in order. All these things are part of the material world we live in and the way we live our material life is a reflection of our spiritual journey. A certain amount of disorder in your home or workplace is acceptable but an extremely cluttered and untidy living space will block the flow of the Force. It is the same with personal finances.

Money is not the root of all evil for a Jediist. Far from it. Money can do a great deal of good in the world and having lots of it may be a sign of spiritual abundance as money is energy like everything else. Money is only evil or negative if you over-value it or think it is an indicator of your self-worth or status.

A Jediist helps others if it is within his or her means, but they certainly don't renounce all worldly things or put their material needs last. Think about it. If you give everything away to the homeless you become the charity case you are trying to prevent. If someone has fallen into a pit of lava, no point jumping in with them. The best way to help others is when you are in control and coming from a position of strength and stability, physically, emotionally and materially.

We live in a material world, but money will not bring you joy and fulfilment, and for proof of that just look at the lives of unhappy celebrities and lottery winners. This isn't to say earning money isn't important. Money is nothing more than a tool to get what we need and to live.

A Jediist helps others if it is within their means.

So, earn enough to buy what you need but don't devalue yourself if you aren't earning millions. Be aware of what money comes in and what goes out. Many people don't keep track of their spending and aimlessly buy stuff they don't need. A Jediist doesn't need stuff to feel they are of value. They know they are enough without stuff to validate them.

DOWN TO EARTH

This chapter has really been about coming down to Earth in our bodies after our travels to galaxies and infinite possibilities far away in previous chapters. It is also about evolving into higher versions of ourselves and that evolution is not just a spiritual one but a physical or material one too.

I was simply too young in 2007 when I founded the church. I needed to grow from boy to man and realize for myself that I had to become the mental, physical, emotional and spiritual change I wanted to see. I'm 31 years old as this book goes to print and certainly feel more mature and ready to take on any challenge with courage, but I remain humble. I remain humble because I know now that I will never stop learning and growing up again and again as, to risk repeating myself, the life of a Jediist is constant spiritual evolution.

LESSON EIGHT: HEALTHY LIVING

Read silently or, better still for the energizing and ritualizing impact, read out loud to yourself the following teaching and then incorporate the practical suggestions into your daily life. Making a commitment to those suggestions is essential otherwise this book is nothing but ideas and words. Too many people get stuck in the "thinking about it" stage but never find the courage or the discipline to do anything about their grand ideas. A Jediist has courage; a Jediist has self-discipline; and a Jediist will also live or embody what he or she believes. If you are to evolve into a Jediist you must move from theory to action as soon as possible. You must both be and do. There is no "I could" or "I might".

The Eighth Teaching on the Force

As Jediists our focus is naturally on the spiritual, but we need to remember that the Force flows within our bodies as well as around us. We also need to remind ourselves that it is in our physical bodies that we live our spiritual lives on Earth.

It is so easy to make excuses for not taking care of your health. We are too busy, or have no time to exercise or cook properly, or the needs of others must come before our own, and so on. Let me tell you that for every excuse you make to neglect your physical health there is a far more powerful reason to consider it. For example, the Force does not flow strongly through you if your health is poor. If you don't eat healthily and exercise, your thinking will be sluggish. If you want to inspire others to live healthy lives you need to set an example, and the healthier you are the easier it is for you to help and inspire others.

Your body is a temple for the Force within you. When you are out of shape physically it is extremely difficult to be spiritually alert and to walk in harmony with the Force. Take control of your body and make it a finely tuned instrument for the Force. Treat your body with the respect and reverence it deserves. Live the Force that is within and all around you. From this day forward make every food, exercise and lifestyle choice one that moves you in perfect harmony with the Force.

Taking care of their body and leading a healthy lifestyle is how a Jediist demonstrates to the world their loving relationship between themselves and their spirit. Putting yourself in the centre of your life is not selfish; it is deeply spiritual. It is an act of love. It is putting your relationship with the Force firmly centre stage.

Self-love is understanding that everyone and everything in your life is not the healer or the salvation for your hurts and wounds. Other people can be messengers alerting you to your wounds but never healers of those wounds. The only person who can heal your life is you. A Jediist looks deep within and discovers within their centre the love and meaning that others waste their lives seeking outside themselves, in other people or material things. A Jediist knows happiness and meaning can never be found on the outside, and the only path to the Force is within.

A lot of people think the world is a competitive place and there is no point even trying as there are always going to be people who do things better than they do, but all of us are exactly the same. Being born with exquisite cheekbones, money and connections does not necessarily give you an advantage. In some instances it can be a curse. The key is to realize that you are infinite possibility, whatever your background, age or stage in life, and you truly can do anything you want when your body, mind and spirit are in harmony with the Force. What other people think does not matter in the slightest. All that matters is your relationship with yourself. Are you feeling happy, fulfilled and joyful? Does your life have meaning? If the answer is no, you must tune into the Force and then find the courage to make your own choices.

The choices of many people are defined by the expectations of others but we all reach a point in our lives, perhaps triggered by a major life event or the loss of a loved one or heartbreak, when we start to feel the need to look within and find out who we are. The sooner that awakening happens the better, because when it does, our spiritual growth begins in earnest and we begin to see that we are in charge of our bodies, our minds, our hearts and our lives. We choose the kind of life we lead, just as we choose what thoughts and feelings we have. Sadly, a lot of people delay or avoid that spiritual awakening: it can feel frightening or lonely becoming an original, rather than following or copying others, or doing what is expected of you. The result is a crisis in middle age or later life when they suddenly realize something is missing and that there has to be more to life.

The older you get, the harder it can be to transform your life, because you become more set in your ways. You are also more likely to have responsibilities and perhaps those who are dependent on you, such as children or elderly relatives. A Jediist takes care of those who are vulnerable and helpless. This isn't to say change is impossible because it is very possible, just harder. Jediism helps all its followers, whatever age they are, understand who they are. It gives them the tools to help them make healthy and positive choices. It helps them understand that they have the power to create the life of their dreams and that true meaning can only be found by taking the road less travelled or by looking within.

Take a moment now to bow your head and focus on the words of this Jediist prayer.

A JEDIIST PRAYER FOR HEALTH IN MIND, BODY AND SPIRIT

May the Force free all beings plagued with sufferings of body and mind from illness and pain, and may all those who feel caged and restricted become free.

May those who have no power find their inner power, and may people think of befriending one another.

May those who find themselves alone and directionless and lost, whether young or old in years, and all those who feel lost find their meaning in the Force. Let us all fill our hearts with love and compassion for ourselves and all living beings. Let us pray that all living beings realize that they are all brothers and sisters, all nourished from the same source of life.

May you know that the journey of your life is the meaning you seek and if you live your life with love and compassion in your heart and nurture your connection to the Force in body, mind, heart and spirit you are already walking the path of the Jediist.

HEALTHY LIVING GUIDELINES

1. Watch and grow

In a chapter dedicated to the importance of healthy diet and regular exercise for spiritual growth it may surprise you that I'm going to recommend some movies because too much screen time isn't ideal. However, moderation in everything is the Jediist code, and if the viewing choices you make expand your mind, or fill you with joy or a sense of curiosity and wonder, they can easily be incorporated into a healthy lifestyle. After all, every *Star Wars* movie falls into this category and without *Star Wars* this book would not have been written. Assuming you are all familiar with the *Star Wars* movies the next three films I'm going to recommend are all relevant to the theme of this chapter but they are also mind-opening and I urge you to make time for them.

My first recommendation is one of my all-time favourite movies. It is a 1999 American film starring Brad Pitt called *Fight Club* and it's a brilliant satire on the culture of consumerism, lifestyle branding and constructions of masculinity. If I haven't convinced you to stop buying things you really don't need, believing that if you buy stuff it can make you feel a certain way, then this film will. An absolute must-watch.

Another movie recommendation which turns the spotlight on subliminal messages to buy and conform that are transmitted to us by the media and advertising is a less well-known film released in 1988 called *They Live*, staring

Roddy Piper. It is the story of a man who discovers that the ruling classes are in fact aliens concealing who they are and manipulating people to accept this situation through subliminal messages in the mass media.

My third movie recommendation may appear contradictory because it is all about the life of Ray Kroc, the businessman who built McDonald's into the most successful fast food chain in the world. It is a 2016 film called *The Founder*, starring Michael Keaton. Remember, Jediism is all about finding healthy balance and becoming a Jediist does not mean you should never eat fast food again. Having the odd burger or ice cream won't damage you, as long as you don't consume what you know isn't good for you in excess.

The reason I'm recommending this film is that Ray was 51 when he bought McDonald's. This was back in the 1950s, and with people living longer these days 50 back then is equivalent to 70 or so now. If you are over 50 and feel life has passed you by and that you can't make changes or do something amazing with your life because you are too old, you could not be more wrong. There is no age limit on going within and transforming your life as a result. Age is just a number when you are a Jediist. I hope whatever age you are, this book will encourage you to go within and find your meaning, energy and purpose and lightness of spirit.

2. Move in harmony with the Force

The emphasis here is on the word move. If you feel tired and out of shape, you aren't moving enough, so commit to regular exercise. Avoid sitting still for long periods. If you work at a computer all day, be sure to get up and move around every half an hour or so. Our bodies were designed to move, not to be constantly inactive. Stillness is to be cultivated within you, not in your day-to-day life. The world we live in is one of energy and potential and, although regular sleep and rest is important, your body is part of that constant energetic swirl. In addition, exercise boosts the flow of nutrients and oxygen to your brain and stimulates your mind.

3. Learn and grow

Start educating yourself about your food choices. Learn about the nutrients required for an optimum diet and what foods boost brain power and mood, and what foods depress them. Treat your body as a temple and what you offer it with the reverence it deserves.

There are stacks of great resources out there online and in print, but one book I do recommend is *The Optimum Nutrition Bible* by Patrick Holford. As much as possible seek out spiritually pure foods in line with the Force that make you feel healthier, lighter and more focused mentally. Spiritually negative foods have the opposite effect. You don't need a degree in nutrition to know which are the former (fresh fruit and vegetables, lean meat, nuts, beans, etc.) and which fall into the latter (fast foods, ready meals, sweets, fries, red meat, cakes, etc.) Avoid addictive substances such as alcohol, cigarettes and drugs.

You also don't need a degree in nutrition to understand

that being overweight isn't usually healthy. If there are medical or emotional reasons for weight problems then counselling, support and guidance are essential. However, for many of us the reason for weight issues is simply eating too much of the wrong kinds of foods. A Jediist educates themselves about the basics of a healthy diet, and in this day and age finding healthy nutrition information online is easy. Accept that you can't just eat whatever you like and still maintain your weight, and if you are comfort eating, however much you eat your appetite will never be filled. The answer to your problems won't ever be found on your plate but in your heart and spirit. You should eat to live and not live to eat. The Force not food should be your master and guide.

4. Eat mindfully

Many of us eat food without thinking these days. Before I realized how important diet was to my well-being mentally, emotionally and spiritually, I would frequently eat fast food at my computer or eat on the go. My life was littered with empty plates and cardboard-box takeaways. As soon as I started to pay attention to the powerful role food played in my life it became obvious to me that this had to change. I needed to pay attention to what I was putting in my mouth and make eating a sacred and mindful act. I needed to cut out the multitasking and eat free from distraction.

I also realized that slowing down the speed I was chewing had a huge impact. Not only did I taste and enjoy the flavour of my food more but I could notice when I was full. I could tell the difference between eating for the sake of eating, and eating because I was hungry.

This exercise can get you thinking and eating along the right lines. All you need is a grape and a timer. Set a timer to two minutes. Pick up the grape and study it as if you had never seen it before. Touch and feel it. Now hold it to your nose and smell it. When you smell it, does your stomach or your mouth react? Next put the grape in your mouth but don't chew it. Notice how the grape feels on your tongue. Now bite and as you do, pay attention to how many times you have to bite until the grape disintegrates. Pause after a few bites and notice how the taste changes the more you bite. Don't swallow until the timer alerts you that two minutes are up. Just before you swallow, notice the intention to swallow.

Obviously you can't eat everything you put in your mouth like this, but the purpose of the exercise is to try to get you to distinguish between the enjoyment and the necessity of food. It will demonstrate to you that you have absolute control over what you chew and swallow. It will also help you consider how amazing and unique each bite of food is as it can never be eaten by anyone else at another time. This morsel of food, this precious moment, cannot be repeated.

5. Pray, eat, love

Before each meal take a moment to say out loud or in your heart this Jediist grace prayer or a variation on this theme to suit you:

May the Force be with this food and may it provide vital nourishment for body, mind, heart and spirit. Gratitude and blessings for what I am (we are) about to receive.

Making a prayer before each meal is a simple act through which you can strengthen your connection to the Force and express gratitude to the universe for the vital life energy each meal provides you with. Gratitude is a vitamin for the spirit.

I AM A JEDIIST

Dr Carole Griggs is a John F. Kennedy university professor, international speaker, professional coach and consultant, author/writer, and pioneer and leader in the areas of consciousness evolution and human development, and integrative wellness and nutrition (Drcaroleggriggs.com). Last, but by no means least, Dr Griggs is a Jediist Master trainer on the Church of Jediism faculty. Below she explains the importance of holistic health and well-being for a Jediist.

Your body is the vehicle, the very doorway to feeling, seeing, and being fully present to all that you are, and all that you are capable of being. The condition of the body very often affects not only one's physical state of health and vitality, but also one's mental and emotional clarity, inner and outer strength, sense of wisdom and groundedness, and feelings of confidence, focus and purpose.

When the body is in chaos (toxic, inflamed, improperly nourished, out of alignment, deconditioned, etc.) it often encourages the mind and emotions to be more chaotic, and vice versa. So learning to nourish and move the body in ways that create a desirable environment to inhabit allows you to become more fully present, more powerful, nimble and agile, and more in tune with the Force that is within you. Tending to the body is one of the big entryways to feeling at home in your own skin, claiming your power and strength, feeling present, at ease and connected to others, feeling aligned with the Force, and living your fullest potential.

Nourishing foods and purposeful strength and conditioning activities not only have tremendous effects on the human body, but also greatly impact one's overall vitality, fulfilment and quality of life. The condition of the body very often affects one's degree of mental and emotional clarity, state(s) of consciousness, inner and outer strength, and capacity to experience connection to everything.

Our bodies communicate to us quite clearly if we are willing to attend to all of their messages. Be fully embodied. And experience and become the Force that is within you.

Evolution isn't just a theory but the Force working within every cell of your body. The Force brought you here to this page, this moment in your life. It is your time to look within and choose to grow.

Daniel M. Jones

Chapter
NINE

Peaceful
Communication
and Interaction with
Diplomacy

"But how am I to know the good side from the bad?"
"You will know. When you are calm. At peace, passive."

Luke and Yoda, *Star Wars Episode V: The Empire Strikes Back*

In *Return of the Jedi* Luke has made himself a lightsaber, which is a symbolic green, similar to the colour of his Jedi Master Yoda's lightsaber. This shows that Luke's training is complete and he is now empowered and ready to return to his quest.

Strong and determined was very much how I felt in the middle of 2016 when I sensed the time had come to reactivate the Church of Jediism. Armed with greater maturity and inner calm, I truly felt ready to spread the word again. The universe responded to my feelings of readiness by sending me green lights or signs that I was on the right path. That shift to "move forward" green began in the most ordinary but extraordinary of ways.

WAKING UP

One summer afternoon in 2016 I was in my local supermarket buying fruit and vegetables. I saw trolleys being loaded with excess that was destined for the rubbish tip because it was all past its sell-by date. I purchased a few items at a vastly reduced price and felt quite pleased with myself but the extent of the waste – when there are so many hungry people in the world – hit me harder than usual. I left the deserted organic food section and noticed to my disappointment that the alcohol section was packed. As I went to the till I was approached by a talkative man selling a broadband deal. It was almost impossible to get past him as he was so insistent and when I finally did he swooped onto the next customer. To make matters worse, on the other side of the aisle there was a woman enthusiastically selling cellphone coverage. I heard her explain to potential customers how the coverage her company offered was far superior to their competitors'.

In that moment I knew with every part of my being that it was time to reawaken Jediism. It was time to offer people the opportunity to look beyond the material and a competitive mindset for a sense of meaning. From birth, the message society gives us is that it's "survival of the fittest" but in my humble opinion that is so wrong. Yes, we are a hunter species but we are also a gatherer species. We have focused so much on the hunter aspect of our nature but if that was all that defined us, we would have destroyed each other completely centuries ago, as tropical fish do when put in a tank together. We are not naturally competitive. As gatherers we also share food, and help and protect each other, and it is because we are gatherers that we have survived, not because we are hunters.

If you stop and think about it, why is it so important to win, or be wealthier, more successful, more famous or more popular than someone else? If you earn millions, will that push the world forward? In the long run does it really matter what your bank balance is? If you get two or two thousand likes on Facebook, is it going to change a thing? If you don't feel good about yourself, no amount of cash, likes, right swipes, hits or cutting-edge phone technology will give you the inner endorsement you crave.

Far from pushing us to reach our potential, the pervasive competitive mindset current in the world today actually decreases our chances of success, because it makes us think we live in a world of scarcity and not abundance. It makes us think that if one person is successful it somehow lessens or diminishes the chances of success of someone else. It's as if success is a cake with only so many slices and not enough slices for everyone. But a Jediist knows that the universe is one of unlimited potential and there is more than enough success to go around for everyone. We can all have a slice of success because the potential of the universe is endless. Indeed success attracts success. The best way to attract success and happiness into your life is not to try to beat others, but to raise your energy vibration by helping others succeed along with you.

In June 2016 I didn't know exactly when or how it would happen, but in that moment the decision to revive the church was made within me. This time, however, instead of rushing full steam ahead with an aggressive media onslaught, as I did when I launched the church in 2007, I decided simply to let go and trust. I handed my intention over to the universe and stayed calm and alert to opportunities to evolve Jediism.

With my intention firmly set, I sent a request to the universe to send me people I could trust to help me reawaken Jediism. Within a few weeks the universe responded and I started to attract like-minded souls into my life. Some of those like-minded souls are featured in the "I am a Jediist" boxes in this book. You can also seek them out on the church's website office of mission faculty, discussed further in the Appendix. These people come from all walks of life, educational backgrounds and belief systems. The uniting factor is that they all share my vision of an awakened world in harmony with the Force within and all around us. Currently they are working with me to help all who join our church become the Force or the positive and peaceful change they want to see in the world. There is no stopping the movement we have created now. The *Star Wars*-loving connections just keep on happening and momentum for the rebirth of the church of Jediism is growing at a rapid pace. The universe is the limit.

Our dream is to empower people all over the world to look within and discover their inner peace and meaning. This isn't to say that being a Jediist means you will never suffer or face problems again. Being a Jediist does not prevent you from facing times of darkness but it teaches you how to cope with darkness, and use it as a tool to grow and evolve.

Perhaps the most powerful way for a Jediist to deal with darkness is to shine light onto it with thoughts, words and acts of love and light. If you respond with negativity to negativity you just feed the power of the dark side. Diplomacy takes great self-control but a Jediist learns to have that inner control by responding to negativity and tension with humility, humour and peace.

THE WAY OF HUMILITY

Looking back, I can see that I have learned a great deal in my three decades on this amazing planet. I have grown in self-understanding and maturity but most important of all I have learned the vital importance of humility. In the early days of the church I lacked humility and the lack of this brought tension, conflict and confusion into my life. I had to learn how absolutely vital it is for a Jediist to develop humility.

What is humility? Humility is the opposite of arrogance, pride, ego and aggression. You might think that being humble robs a Jediist of his or her power but that could not be further from the truth. Humility gifts you tremendous power because it frees you from the need to impress others or compete against others or get ahead. When you are humble you see everything and everyone in this life as an opportunity to learn and grow. Remember, being a Jediist is all about learning and evolving into higher versions of yourself.

It is possible to have self-esteem but also remain humble. Self-esteem without humility is arrogance, and arrogance closes minds because you think you know everything and shut the door to new perspectives. By remaining humble you remain open to the possibility of improvement. You also feel empathy and love for all human life because you understand that we are all connected. No one person is greater or less than another.

When you are humble you respect the opinions of others; you listen more and speak less. You do not judge others and you understand that happiness can never be found in always being right or always winning. True contentment is found in helping others grow and in savouring the journey rather than focusing only on the destination.

Humility begins from the heart. It does not try to prove itself to others but has everything to offer others. Humility is the hallmark of a true Jediist.

By remaining humble you remain open to the possibility of improvement.

THE WAY OF GOOD HUMOUR

Along with humility a Jediist will approach life with a lightness of spirit, knowing that joy can defuse tension. Perhaps the most wonderful quality about Jediism is that for whatever reason it makes people smile. If you don't believe me, start talking about Jediism with someone you know and see what their first response is. In the great majority of cases you will see that it triggers a good-humoured response. You may even notice that people get a far-away look in their eyes. This is them reconnecting to their inner child.

I love seeing this beautiful reaction because spirituality should be about joy. A Jediist should bring lightness of spirit into the world. Nothing dissolves conflict better than good-

TAKE AN APPRENTICE

As Yoda says in *Return of the Jedi*, "pass on what you have learned". Once you start to feel calmer, and more collected and disciplined, because you are learning to look within yourself rather than outside yourself for meaning, others will notice the difference in you and the way you react to situations and life in general. You will become someone other people admire or want to follow. I've seen that happen many times within my church. A new member joins and learns and grows in self-awareness and confidence, and the world responds to them differently. They gradually gain followers and new friends. If this happens to you don't feel "less than" or that you are not worthy – rise to the challenge. Set an example and share your newfound calm and wisdom with others or better still take on an apprentice to guide and nurture. Passing on your knowledge and helping another person find inner peace is one of the most rewarding things about following the way of the Jediist. Inspiring, helping and guiding is the way of the Jediist.

natured humour. It's impossible to fear or hate someone or something when you inject a little humour. Humour can unite where tension divides. A Jediist thinks lightly of him or herself but deeply of the universe.

Glancing back at my life as a Jediist there have been some tough and challenging times but also countless funny times. In every case these moments of lightness have eased tension and reminded me what truly matters in life. Laughter has often grounded me and brought me right back to Earth when I need reminding how important humility is. It has also created or strengthened loving bonds. Let me give a couple of examples.

I remember a few years ago staying in a hotel in Kent with my cousin. I'd done a series of interviews for radio and TV shows. The interviews had gone particularly well and I went to bed feeling very pleased with myself. I'd been asked to sign several autographs that day. I loved signing autographs.

I fell asleep but woke up in the middle of the night to the sound of a loud bang coming from the window. My instant reaction was to think it must be a deranged fan stalking me. I shouted to my cousin to call the police. I was terrified, but adrenalin and survival mode kicked in. I leaped out of bed. I didn't have any weapon to protect me and in my panic the only thing I could find was a replica lightsaber. I grabbed it and headed towards the banging noise to confront what I was convinced was a stalker...

Suddenly, the light switched on and I heard my cousin howling with laughter. I turned around to look at him and he was literally rolling about on the floor. I then realized why he was laughing. I was standing in the middle of the room in my underpants with a lightsaber in my hand. What use would that lightsaber have been? As for my obsessive stalker – it was simply a blind that had not been folded away properly. Pride certainly comes before a fall.

Another occasion when I found myself laughing uncontrollably because I had a lightsaber in my hand happened a few years ago when none other than *Star Wars* actor Warwick Davis, who played the Ewok Wicket, visited my house. Warwick had found out about the Church of Jediism at a comic book convention and got in touch to ask if he could feature Jediism on his *Weekend Escapes* TV show. On his TV show I knighted him and made him an honoured life-time member of the Church of Jediism. To celebrate his initiation we had a spontaneous pretend lightsaber battle in my garden. The laughter we shared that day created a bond between us that remains unbroken to this day.

Laughter is a great healer, teacher and communicator. It is the diplomatic weapon of choice for every Jediist.

THE WAY OF PEACE

Peaceful communication and interaction with diplomacy is the way forward for the world. It is a defining feature of the relaunched Church of Jediism – which accepts people of all religions and beliefs systems, believing the Force flows within and around all of us regardless of what we do or not believe. A Jediist never loses hope that peace, light and love will conquer darkness. In his final moments even Darth Vader (the personification of darkness) shows a softer side, a heart that is dying but still beating with love for his son, a love he has denied not just to his son but to himself. A Jediist believes that there is always light to be found, even in the darkest places. They focus all of their intentions on finding that light.

I urge all of you to focus your intentions on the light side of the Force. Think it, feel it and become it. Be the humble, light-hearted and peaceful change you want to see in the world. Do not lose yourself in the storm. Be the calm in the storm. Trust in the Force always. It will guide and inspire you when you learn to seek peace from the inside out.

Discover your deep inner calm and from there spread love, light and compassion in every direction. The way of inner peace is the way of the Jediist. You are a Jediist. You are living peace and a warrior of the light.

LESSON NINE: PEACEFUL LIVING

Read silently or, better still for the energizing and ritualizing impact, read out loud to yourself the following teaching and then incorporate the practical suggestions into your daily life. Making a commitment to those suggestions is essential otherwise this book is nothing but ideas and words. Too many people get stuck in the "thinking about it" stage but never find the courage or the discipline to do anything about their grand ideas. A Jediist has courage; a Jediist has self-discipline; and a Jediist will also live or embody what he or she believes. If you are to evolve into a Jediist you must move from theory to action as soon as possible. You must both be and do. There is no "I could" or "I might".

The Ninth and Final Teaching on the Force

It is a blessing to have your attention. Of course, I know that I can't have your 100 per cent attention during this teaching because sometimes your mind is going to drift. But when it does drift I'd like to encourage you to let it drift towards gratitude.

Attitude can define us. Choosing gratitude as our attitude may be the single most important positive decision we make every day of our lives. The grateful person knows that the Force is with them and they give thanks for that. Ingratitude is born in the dark side of the Force. It makes us believe that other people owe us something or that something is missing from our lives. Grateful people live their lives in ways that say thank you to the Force. They are humble and take nothing in this amazing world for granted. Grateful people are victors and not victims, because they know that we cannot always control what happens to us in life or what we receive, but we can always choose how we respond. They choose to focus on what they have to be thankful for, even if that is only the ability to choose what we think and how we respond.

So choose gratitude and humility instead of resentment and conflict even when the world feels dark. If people criticize or hurt you without cause, thank them for showing you a dark path in life you don't want to follow. If people try to influence others against you, be grateful as you don't want people in your life who are so easily swayed against you. If you encounter disappointment, or feel sad or anxious, be grateful for what that experience or feeling teaches you. Give thanks that you are blessed with the power of choice and can always choose love and compassion towards yourself and others. Always focus on what you have to give thanks for and what you can use to build towards the future. This is how to make the most of life rather than just the best of it.

We take too much for granted and don't appreciate what we have until it is gone. To become a Jediist is to become a person who is eternally humble and thankful for his or her blessings. A Jediist doesn't expect the world to owe them a living. A Jediist is grateful for what they already have and doesn't crave to have more than they need because they know that all they need can be found within. In a world that is becoming increasingly selfish and dependent, this independent and content stance makes a Jediist stand out from the crowd. Indeed, it is always possible to recognize when you encounter a Jediist. You will know they are a Jediist at heart because after spending time with them you will feel lighter and happier. A Jediist transmits their quiet, grateful, humble joy in living and their inner peace to others. They are warriors of the light.

Thankfulness is more than a prayer or a wish or a feeling; it is essential for living in harmony with the Force, because an attitude of gratitude nurtures humility and builds internal tranquillity. When you give thanks for every situation you encounter in your life, because you know you will learn and grow in some way, you are truly at peace. When you are grateful you will feel light. Your heart will open. You become the Force. Your face will shine and your eyes will brighten, and others will be attracted to you. When you feel grateful you will see the Force within everyone and everything. When you feel grateful you are at peace because you have become peace. You are a light and a blessing to the world.

Take a moment now to ponder the words of this Jediist prayer for peace.

A JEDIIST PRAYER FOR INNER PEACE

May the Force bring me peace, the deep inner peace that stays deep in my heart by day and by night.

May I know that fear is an illusion and that it has no place in my life. Most of what I fear does not come to pass and simply exists in my head. I will let go of those fears and put my faith in the Force within me and all around. I will admit that I can't control other people, plans or even what happens to me, but I can control how I respond and focus with gratitude on what is good. I can feel gratitude for every blessing I have received. If I just let go and trust I will experience peace that surpasses all understanding. That is the peace of the Jediist and it is the peace that is my destiny.

The next time I feel anxious or worried or stressed, may I from this day forward remember to connect to the power of the living life Force within me and all around me as it is the only way to calm my fears.

May the Force not only bring me peace but be my peace in any situation.

And whenever I connect to the Force – in this prayer, in helping others, in counting my blessings, in choosing to interact with peace and diplomacy – may I feel the power of the Force grow ever stronger and ever more powerful within me, always and forever.

PEACEFUL AND DIPLOMATIC LIVING GUIDELINES

1. Learn to listen

Talking is a natural skill but effective communication needs to be learned. One of the biggest causes of disagreement is people simply not listening to each other. The way of the Jediist is to allow people to express their thoughts and feelings without constantly interrupting with your thoughts. If you listen to others they are more likely to listen to you. Really listen when others speak. Don't think about what your response will be while they are speaking, and try to avoid criticizing and advising unless your opinion is requested. Be reflective in your listening. Restating or reflecting back what others say to you shows you have been listening and is a mark of respect to them. Don't be afraid of silence as it gives you and the other person a chance to gather your thoughts. A great deal can be said in times of silence: "I'm listening. I'm understanding. I'm there for you."

2. Say what you mean and be true to your word

When you communicate with others, be as honest and direct as possible. Say what you mean but without causing offence. In other words, be diplomatic. Don't tell someone you don't like their haircut; tell them you don't think this particular cut flatters them enough. If someone has done something to offend you, focus on the feelings it arouses in you in such a way as to not make the other person feel they are to blame. So you don't blame the person but focus attention on your feelings. For example, say, "When you said that, it made me feel anxious," instead of, "You are making me feel anxious."

3. Be gently assertive

A Jediist is gently assertive. They respond to others in a way that does not undermine them or other people. They know what they want, decide if what they want is fair to everyone involved, and ask for it calmly and clearly. A Jediist will remain objective, calm and focused during tense dialogues. They will see all sides of a situation and recognize both their own needs as well as the needs of others. Their aim is not to win an argument but to find a harmonious way forward that works for everyone.

If someone tries to undermine you with criticism, first of all see if they have a point, and if they do, learn from it and be grateful to that person for pointing it out. If, however, the criticism is hurtful, bear in mind that this often means you are worthy of their time and attention so you may want to take it as a compliment.

If people constantly take advantage of your giving and loving nature, it is time to start being more assertive. It is okay to say no to unreasonable requests. If you are helping others because you really want to and don't feel diminished in any way by offering that help, that is fine, carry on as you are. But if you are helping because you are frightened people won't like you if you say no, remind yourself that those who truly care about you will not put unwelcome demands on you. If you start feeling obligated or guilty in your relationships, then it is time to change the dynamic of your relationships, because they should be based on free will, love and mutual respect. Think about it this way: if you knew your friends and family only did things for you because they felt they ought to and not because they loved you, would you want them to feel that way about you?

Communication with diplomacy is understanding and not hurting others. It is considering the impact of your words. Research has shown just how much power words have to inflict harm and damage on plants and I truly believe they can do the same to humans. Being someone with Asperger's, I can't intuitively sense how my words impact others so I have had to research, study and learn. My approach is always to try to be diplomatic, reasonable and pleasant because if you do that you can't go wrong. You also never truly know what is going on in the life of the person you are talking to – they could be struggling with personal issues or in extreme cases just diagnosed with a serious illness or lost a loved one – so don't ever take what people say to you personally. At all times use your words to empower others, and avoid negativity and gossip as it serves no purpose but to energize the darkness. Never forget, a Jediist is a being of light and a bringer of light.

4. Constantly create

If you want to experience life fully, stop copying what others have done before and create instead. A Jediist is infinite creativity. That is our natural state. Bring your own creativity to your work and your hobbies or interests. Get advice from experts then put your own unique stamp on how you practise or perform it. Don't tell yourself you can't do or learn something because you aren't an expert, or clever, original or young enough. You are what you think you are, and in this day and age with so much information available for free online, you can learn about virtually anything. And when it comes to originality remember there is nobody on this planet like you, with your DNA, and there is never going to be someone like you ever again. You are born an original miracle and creativity is your birthright. There is no one else in the world who is you and that is your power.

5. Pay attention to coincidences

Coincidences, or synchronicity to give them their spiritual name, are the language the Force speaks. Time and time again in my life I know that when I am at peace with myself things just seem to happen at the right time or I meet the right people to help me move forward. In other words unexpected things just fall into place at the right time, which is the definition of synchronicity.

After I made the decision to reactivate the church and surrendered the "how this would happen" to the universe, I felt the Force at work through a series of wonderful coincidences that brought a team of dedicated and heartfelt people into my life to help me make it happen.

So, the next time you find yourself thinking "that was a coincidence" or marvelling at the perfection of how things have just happened or fallen into place, take a moment to reflect and be still. It's a clear sign from the universe that the Force is with you and you are on the right path.

6. Don't fight with anyone

A Jediist avoids conflict and retaliation because he or she knows that if a person is unjustly unkind or hurtful they are speaking from a position of personal pain and confusion and won't be ready to hear anything. They also trust that the universal law of karma – actions are all eventually rewarded and punished by the universe – will take care of them. When confronted by someone unreasonable a Jediist will not react and will remain calm. They will send love and forgiveness to the other person and in the process become the Force.

There will be times when you simply can't turn a blind eye and that is when you see extreme examples of cruelty or injustice to those who are defenceless, vulnerable and can't defend themselves. In those cases a Jediist will not remain silent or passive because these are instances that truly matter. A Jediist will always defend the vulnerable and defenceless. It is a matter of degree. With self-awareness and inner calm a Jediist will know what and who is worth fighting and standing up for and what isn't.

7. Flex your gratitude muscle

This simple five-minute exercise repeated for seven days in a row can bring remarkable feelings of contentment and inner calm.

For the next seven days write down three things in your day that went well then add a one-sentence explanation for each about why it went well. Taking the time consciously to express gratitude in writing helps us remember what we already have in our lives. It's worth making this "three good things today" exercise a habit or sacred ritual because generating gratitude is an underdeveloped skill, and the more you practise, the better you will get. The more you choose gratitude, the more peace there will be in your life. It's even possible to be thankful for those times when you feel low or annoyed with yourself. The fact that you are annoyed shows that you are aware there is a problem and, when you are aware, you are empowered because you can choose to make a change.

I AM A JEDIIST

Andrew Nielsen, professional name MC Lars, is an American rapper. He is one of the originators of "it-hop" and one of the first rappers to sample and reference post-punk bands. I first met Lars when he was on tour in the UK in 2007 and we have remained friends ever since, bonding over our mutual love of pop punk and Star Wars. A few years later my band Straight Jacket Legends collaborated with Lars on a song called "She's out of Line", which you can find on YouTube. Then in 2013/14 we went on tour together.

Lars is a true Jediist in heart and spirit. Two years ago – and encouraged by me – he wrote a rap about being a Jedi for his

Zombie Dinosaur *LP album. You can find that rap on YouTube but he gave the Church of Jediism his full and joyful permission to print the lyrics below. He feels those lyrics perfectly sum up his thinking about the wonders of being a Jediist far better than any essay he could write. You'll notice that the lyrics are light-hearted. Laughter is so often missing from religion and spirituality when it should be at the heart of it. Jediism hopes to inject the "enjoy" part back into modern spirituality. Lars' rap is a great place to start:*

"If I Were a Jedi (That Would be Hella Awesome)"
MC Lars
Featuring Brian Mazzaferri of I Fight Dragons
Music by MC Lars, Brandon Arnovick, Watt White and the
    Kickstarter homies
Lyrics by MC Lars and Watt White

This beat is my recital, I think it's very vital
To use (the force) for good (of course)
Lars Skywalker that's my title! (here we go!)
If I were a Jedi, I could out-rap Busta Rhymes
Going in like Qui-Gon Jinn for the win, I could flow in quadruple
    time
And at the Canadian border, every time I went on tour
I'd be like "this is not the undeclared MC Lars merch that you're
    looking for"
I could levitate like Yoda, I'd eradicate ebola
I could pick up girls, literally, even master the viola

I could read all of *War and Peace* in ten minutes

Entirely in Russian just to say that I did it

I could even catch that golden snitch playing Quidditch

(Wait, wrong movie, innit?)

Podracing up the 101, surpassing Golden Gate traffic (whoo!)

R2 on the roof of my Prius (dude), I could FaceTime holographic

I'd play for the A's and we'd win every game

Resurrect Mac Dre do it all for the Bay

They'd all say hey Lars is neato

And always let me cut the line at El Farrolito

Two years ago, a friend of mine

Asked me to say some Jedi rhymes

So I said this rhyme, I'm about to say

I fought the Sith and it went this way

CHORUS:

If I were a Jedi, bet I'd get all the ladies

I would mack it more than Dumbledore or Leto Atreides

If you try to strike me down I'll just be more powerful

If I were a Jedi, that would be hella awesome

(Singin'!)

Do or do not there is no try!

Do or do not there is no try!

Do or do not, there is no try!

And if you don't believe it you will fail every time

It's a trap! (x2)

Hey! Hey! Hey! Hey! Hey! Hey! Hey!

It's a trap!

Choose peace and you will become peace.

Daniel M. Jones

EPILOGUE

Not the End

Mind what you have learned. Save you it can.

Yoda, *Star Wars Episode V: The Empire Strikes Back*

The moment you understand that the way forward is to look within yourself for answers, you realize that any hindrances you face are caused by your disconnection from your inner being. In other words, not making friends with yourself is the enemy or the dark side of the Force at work. Your inner being is what makes you who you are. It is all-powerful, intelligent, all-loving and wise. You can call this spirit or the Force within you. It doesn't matter what you call it. The important thing is you know that you are more than your body or external appearances. You are an eternal spiritual being in human form. You are the Force and can change your life by changing your thoughts, and the way your focus attracts people and situations to you.

Self-help and independence of spirit is the way of the Jediist. Overcoming personal struggles can awaken you to your purpose, which is to bring light, love, peace and harmony into the world. Every time a Jediist seeks meaning from within and consciously chooses peace and love, the light side of the Force grows stronger. It is entirely plausible that the Jediist-minded among us today can usher in a new spirituality and shift in global consciousness towards peace and harmony that is more powerful than any we can possibly imagine.

I hope what you have read in this book will have shown you that Jediism is not so much a religion but an exciting and relevant spiritual or philosophical movement – a universal desire for self-awareness, awakening, peace, love and harmony that is alive within us all whatever our age, background, culture, religion or belief system. It is about recognizing that spark of desire within ourselves and others, and seeing how that desire interconnects us all. It is attracting success and happiness and a deep sense of meaning and purpose into your life. It is empowering mind, body, heart and spirit. It is knowing you are in control of your life but also having the ability to let go when things cannot be changed and trusting that the universe will bring you what you need at the right time.

Jediism is embodying love, gratitude and peace and remaining humble, because no Jediist can know all there is to be known about the Force as it is beyond our understanding on Earth. We can only surrender to its mystery and trust that everything happens for a reason, even the bad. A Jediist stays strong during dark times by remembering who they are and no matter what happens always keeping their heart and mind facing the light.

FINDING YOUR WAY

When I founded Jediism in 2007 it wasn't the right time to launch Jediism and its powerful message of self-awakening. Initially the movement was a religion with rituals and clothing requirements, but it has grown and changed and left all those unnecessary material concerns behind. Everything I have learned these last ten years has transformed it into a philosophical and spiritual movement rather than a religion. It's a whole new world out there.

Increasingly, people aren't looking to religion for a sense of meaning. We are all starting to ask questions and demand answers rather than quietly accepting what we are told or what is expected of us. If one of those questions you ask yourself is: "What is the meaning of my life?" or "How can I find my meaning?", Jediism is here to help you find your answers.

In this book I've presented the nine lessons I learned about how to live as a Jediist Master. I hope you will come to think of this book as your arrow to the Force within and around you. I hope it will be a book that you will return to time and again for inspiration, guidance, comfort and a sense of meaning. Be aware, though, that your journey as a Jediist doesn't end here on this page. This book has barely scratched the surface of who you are and what you are here to do. It is only the beginning. There is so much more for you to learn and I hope you will never stop discovering yourself and creating the life of your dreams. I hope you will continue your journey of spiritual awakening and evolution by joining the Church of Jediism. (Details about how to do that can be found in the Appendix.)

Whether you decide to join the church or not, I hope this book has opened your mind to new possibilities and reminded you that there is so much more to you and this life than meets the eye. Remember, the way of the Jediist will take you to a place that is not on any map, but to an unseen galaxy of creativity, power and love you never knew existed within and all around you.

If you want to live a meaningful life you are already a Jediist at heart. It's your life. Follow your heart...

Find yourself by becoming the Force.

Daniel M. Jones

APPENDIX

A New Way in Faith

1. Daniel's Jediist Library Recommendations
2. Census Appeal
3. The Church of Jediism
   - About the Church of Jediism
   - How to Join
   - Connecting with the Church
4. The Church of Jediist Technology
5. Becoming a Jediist Master

1

Daniel's Jediist Library Recommendations

I refer to the books below in the text; I have given the most recent versions available, but enjoy the process of seeking your own guides.

The Book of Proverbs by King Solomon, from King James Bible, Collins, 2011

Brown, Dan, *The Lost Symbol*, Corgi, 2010

Chopra, Deepak, *The Path to Love: Spiritual Strategies for Healing*, Three Rivers Press, 1998

Clark, Angus, *Tai Chi: A Practical Approach to the Ancient Chinese Movement for Health and Well-Being*, Element, 2002

Collard, Patrizia, *The Little Book of Mindfulness: 10 Minutes a Day to Less Stress, More Peace*, Gaia, 2014

de Pape, Baptist, *The Power of the Heart: Finding Your True Purpose in Life*, Atria Books, 2014

Edelman, Sarah, *Change Your Thinking with CBT: Overcome Stress, Combat Anxiety and Improve Your Life*, Vermillion, 2006

Giacobbe, Guilio Cesare, *How to Become a Buddha in 5 Weeks: The Simple Way to Self-Realisation*, Arcturus Publishing, Ltd, 2009

Hobbs, Nicola Jane, *Yoga Gym: The Revolutionary 28 Day Bodyweight Plan: For Strength, Flexibility and Fat Loss*, Bloomsbury, 2015

Holford, Patrick, *The Optimum Nutrition Bible: The Book You Have to Read if You Care about Your Health*, Piatkus, 2004

Lao Tzu, *Tao te Ching*, Create Space Independent Publishing, 2017

Moore, A., *The Complete Guide to Cosmic Ordering*, Bookmart Ltd, 2006

Mutwa, Vusamazulu Credo, *Zulu Shaman: Dreams, Prophecies and Mysteries,* Destiny Books, 2003

Peck, M. Scott, *The Road Less Travelled*, Arrow, 1990

Plato, *The Republic*, Penguin Classics, 2007

Rider, Carl, *Your Psychic Power: A Practical Guide to Developing Your Natural Clairvoyant Abilities*, Piatkus, 1988

Saint Augustine, *The Confessions of St Augustine*, Oxford World Classics, 2008

Smith, James, *You Are What You Love: The Spiritual Power of Habit*, Brazos Press, 2016

Sun Tzu, *The Art of War*, Pax Librorum, 2009

Taylor, Steve, *Making Time: Why Time Seems to Pass at Different Speeds and How to Control It*, Icon Books, 2008

Watts, Alan, *The Book: On the Taboo Against Knowing Who You Are*, Souvenir Press, 2009

Williamson, Marianne, *A Return to Love: Reflections on the Principles of "A Course in Miracles"*, Harper Thorsons, 2015

2

Census Appeal

If you are reading this and you were one of those free-spirited people who for whatever reason listed "Jedi" or "Jedi Knight" as your religion on the 2001 census, or any census, I do hope you will get in touch with me. There may have been a reason why you did that. I would love to hear your story. Details of how to contact me and how to join the Church of Jediism if you feel inspired can be found on the next page.

3

The Church of Jediism

If you have read the book to this point it's very possible you are a Jediist at heart and you want to take control of your life and be a force for positive change in the world. I truly hope you will join the Church of Jediism and become a practitioner by following the five-pillar training programme offered there. Then, once you have completed your training you will pass your wisdom on to others, because helping others is what Jediists do. In this way we change the world, one Jediist at a time, starting with you.

About the Church of Jediism

The international Church of Jediism connects people from all backgrounds and ages with one goal and that is to understand the true meaning of their lives and discover their full potential. You don't have to change your religion or drop a certain belief (some Jediists are deeply religious, others are atheists) or even have an in-depth knowledge of the *Star Wars* universe to become a part of the Church of Jediism. We are here to help you awaken and find your own unique path to your own unique truth by offering you suggestions and signposts rather than commands.

When you join our church you will find that we believe in infinite possibilities, and we work with you and offer training and guidelines to change your life for the better. We promote the path of harmony with the Force through finding happiness by helping others. One day, if enough of us become the Force, we will have created a New World in which there is no discrimination, no violence, no cruelty and no poverty. The Church of Jediism is focused on unifying people all over the world in order to help them learn how to use the power of the Force within and around them to achieve this goal.

How to Join

At present the Church of Jediism is an online movement. If you would like to join our online community, simply go to www.becometheforce.com or www.thechurchofjediism.org and follow the instructions there.

Once you register at our website you can download free literature, join our forums, visit our shop and Jediist technology portal, and find all relevant links to the Church of Jediism on Facebook, Instagram, Twitter and our YouTube channel. You can connect to me, the Jediist Master Office of Mission Administration team working for the church and our team of highly skilled Jediist Master trainers, who look forward to working with you through the five-pillar training programme. This programme isn't compulsory when you join the website but will give you all the tools, techniques, guidance and inspiration you need to become a Jediist Master and play a more active role in the church if you feel that is your destiny.

Connecting with the church

All email addresses are on the website but if you prefer to make an initial inquiry before joining the website you can email me or any of the Church of Jediism team with specific questions by using their first name and adding @churchofjediism.com. Depending on volume of email traffic please allow up to 14 days for a reply:

Daniel@thechurchofjediism.org

(Jediist Master, founding head and inspiration)

Kenn@thechurchofjediism.org

(Jediist Master, website creation and design)

Theresa@thechurchofjediism.org

(Jediist Master, writer and researcher)

You can also inquire in person about the Church of Jediism by visiting the Watkins Books shop in Cecil Court, Leicester Square, London, or in writing to:

Watkins Media
Unit 11
Shepperton House
89–93 Shepperton Road
London
N1 3DF

or the American Event and Literature Center at:

EarthRise Transformative Learning and Retreat Center

101 San Antonio Road

Petaluma

California

USA

djonsson@noetic.org

Tel: +1 (707) 779-8202

www.noetic.org/earthrise/virtual-tour

Recommended visit:

College of Psychic Studies

16 Queensberry Place

London

SW7 2EB

UK

www.collegeofpsychicstudies.co.uk

4

The Church of Jediist Technology

The Church of Jediism was founded online, and Jediists use and harness online technology as spiritual aids. Like the Force, the online world has a dark and a light side but as Jediists we always focus on the light. We regard the internet as a tremendously exciting force for education, progress and for good, and it can become a force for positive transformation if enough Jediist-minded people are involved in it.

We live in an online world and the spiritual revolution will occur online and so we encourage all new members to become internet fluent and to learn about technology and app development. Our website has a specialist Jediist technology portal with Jediist apps and progressive self-development apps we endorse as well as opportunities for members to develop their technology skills and create and develop their own Jediist apps with us.

5

Becoming a Jediist Master

When you join our website there will be levels to progress through that will unlock different features and forums on the site. We do this to encourage learning and self-development, and to ensure that when you progress to another level you have sufficient knowledge and understanding to make the most of that level. The goal of the five-pillar training is to achieve Jediist Master status but as with everything in life the journey is the destination. Our aim on the website is to make that journey engaging and fun and we value and appreciate all your feedback if you decide to work through the five-pillar Jediist Master training programme with us.

Throughout your journey with us there will always be opportunities to connect with the church and fellow Jediists all around the world, as well as myself and the church mission and training teams, to discuss your progress and your dreams. We feel blessed and honoured by your trust in us. We will return that trust by devoting ourselves to helping you awaken your potential and finding your meaning and purpose in life – because when you are awakened you truly do become the Force.

The meaning of your life is to find your meaning. The purpose of your life is to help others.

Daniel M. Jones

NOTES ON THE FORCE

Please use this section of the book to write

    1) a review of this book

    2) a review of your favourite Star Wars *movie*

    3) your thoughts on how you can become the Force.

Choose your favourite write up of the three and then type it up and send it to www.becometheforce.com for possible posting online.

    The reason I'm asking you to write and not type here is that many of us have lost sight of the joy of writing by hand. There is something very immediate and real about it and it will make this book feel uniquely personal and relevant to you. Don't overthink as you write. We look forward to reading what you have to say. Just write straight from your heart and feel the Force speak through you.